LONELINESS

LET'S
TALK
ABOUT

LET'S
TALK
ABOUT
LONELINESS

SIMONE HENG

HAY HOUSE
Carlsbad, California • New York City
London • Sydney • New Delhi

Published in the United Kingdom by:
Hay House UK Ltd, The Sixth Floor, Watson House
54 Baker Street, London W1U 7BU
Tel: +44 (0)20 3927 7290; Fax: +44 (0)20 3927 7291
www.hayhouse.co.uk

Published in the United States of America by:
Hay House Inc., PO Box 5100, Carlsbad, CA 92018-5100
Tel: (1) 760 431 7695 or (800) 654 5126
Fax: (1) 760 431 6948 or (800) 650 5115; www.hayhouse.com

Published in Australia by:
Hay House Australia Ltd, 18/36 Ralph St, Alexandria NSW 2015
Tel: (61) 2 9669 4299; Fax: (61) 2 9669 4144; www.hayhouse.com.au

Published in India by:
Hay House Publishers India, Muskaan Complex,
Plot No.3, B-2, Vasant Kunj, New Delhi 110 070
Tel: (91) 11 4176 1620; Fax: (91) 11 4176 1630; www.hayhouse.co.in

A catalogue record for this book is available from the British Library.

Tradepaper ISBN: 978-1-4019-7488-6
E-book ISBN: 978-1-83782-046-7
Audiobook ISBN: 978-1-83782-045-0

10 9 8 7 6 5 4 3 2 1

Printed in the United States of America

For my parents, Robert and Sandra.

*I know you did the best you could
with what you had at the time.*

*You were both human connection
superheroes in your own way.*

| Contents

| Introduction

My hand is shaking. I cannot take down the TikTok video. I cannot even toggle to the trash bin icon. I've been found out. I'm flushed red and mortified. Shame floods my body. I have put up a video about the first time I learnt to say 'sorry'. The story is about my upbringing in an Asian household, where the word 'sorry' wasn't used. The point of the video is that I was already nineteen when I learnt to say sorry without sarcasm – and that we can learn from unlikely teachers how to become better. The story is meant to be inspirational. It is, until my past comes back to bite me. *I'm a fraud*, I think. *I've been found out.*

A young man writes in my video comments: 'I served you at my store in 2015. You shouted at me. You were the worst customer I had in six years.' I toggle quickly to find his name and add him on Instagram, where I can message him voice notes to apologize. I delete the video. I want to shrink, so small that I disappear. The shame that washes over me and sinks into my veins is like ink dropped in water – it spreads quickly, pervasively. My unlovable past is back to haunt me. For a moment, I'm that girl whose cousin made a group chat on WhatsApp to bitch about her during a bachelorette trip to Bali. For a moment, I'm the girl who never had a pack of friends at high school; the girl who didn't even know herself, so her colleagues couldn't stand her – the girl who didn't know how to love because she wasn't shown enough love herself.

I stop myself. My counselor told me that catastrophizing – jumping to the worst possible conclusion, with or without firm evidence – is part of a trauma response. I breathe. I remember all the self-work and research I've done on connection; my hand stops trembling. I send a voice note to the young man, and I apologize. As I do this, my mind says, *you were the worst kind of shitty, enraged person.* Then my rational brain kicks in and says, *you* were *that person. That person was born in the belly of grief and loneliness. You do better now. GO FIX THIS.*

After counseling myself, I can dialogue with the young man. He watches some of my speeches, and I send him screenshots of messages I'd received when I lived in Dubai, from servicepeople who'd been promoted because I told their managers how amazing they were. I'm trying to prove that the trauma that filled me with rage was a moment in time; my actions weren't my character, and they certainly had nothing to do with him. He forgives me. He tells me I'm so strong to have gone through what I have. Although he forgives me, it takes me weeks until I forgive myself. I'm glad he got in touch; it was a mirror held up to me in the midst of writing this book, reminding me of the 'human' part of 'human connection.' To be human is to be deeply fallible.

You may feel rich with rage. Your trauma is bigger than you. You look at others with envy at the ease with which they view the world. People, for them, aren't a threat. They feel so safe. You can tell just by looking at them. You haven't felt safe in years. They laugh, open-mouthed, at criticism, and it cascades off them like water off the proverbial duck's back. For you, criticism is a painful trigger, like a thorn being ripped out of the flesh of your foot. Like me, your lack of safety could have started by not being soothed by a caregiver or by losing a direct family member when you were young.

By the time my mother's legs stopped working, I felt even less safe. We weren't one of the chosen families where the father bounces back and survives cancer. We weren't one of the chosen families whose mother walks again after a stroke.

I remember when I started very delayed grief therapy. I'd disassociated from the pain of my early years, so it was almost two decades after my father's passing when I finally got to a therapist's office. But better late than never. In therapy, I learnt I needed help, not just to grieve my father's death or my mother's paralysis, but also to heal parts of me wounded much earlier, in my childhood.

My therapist asked me, 'What do you want to get out of this?'

I said, with a mix of self-hatred and envy: 'I want to be one of those easygoing, carefree people.' Those who view comments as feedback, not – as I did – as criticism, every remark a stab wound that needed to be stitched and unstitched, analyzed painfully from every angle. I wanted to be simple. I yearned to be basic.

I wanted to be like the Aussie customers I'd once watched at my father's shop, who replied, 'Can't complain,' to the question, 'How are you?' So laid back, their gratitude so entrenched, or their expectations so small, it could be summed up in two words.

I sat in that counselor's office in my socks, cross-legged on a chair, shoes at the door. My arms crossed around me, embracing myself for fear that I'd fall apart. I thought, *Who are those people?* Those people seemed to live on another planet foreign to us 'trauma babies.' For us, dysfunction was an ever-present shadow in our childhood. *We would never be allowed entry into a smooth, easy existence*, I thought. But that statement, as you'll learn through this book, just wasn't true. I secretly knew that it was untrue; otherwise, why would I have walked to reception and booked my next appointment? I had a small sliver of hope embedded in my gut after that session. I didn't know it yet, but that sliver was human connection.

Have you felt a hint of disconnection from yourself? You may remember your joy as a child: carefree, artistic, and loving. Somewhere, a relative or primary caregiver puts you down. They do it again and again, daily. For those of us who experienced this, it's called a 'little t' trauma, a chipping away at who we are. We talk too loudly, so we're shushed. We gain weight, so we're publicly shamed. We don't get the best grades, so we're destined to be the 'dumb one' in the family.

I hope this book will be your first insight into the fact that you're not alone. I'll speak about things that are felt universally: loneliness in the midst of unprecedented digital connectivity; the legacy of loneliness caused by an isolating pandemic; and the effects of childhood trauma on how we connect with others. I'll also pull back the curtain to reveal things that some of us from an Asian background don't say out loud, let alone put in print. Maybe this will stop you from feeling you have something to be ashamed of, because nothing augments shame like silence.

My hope is that you'll feel less alone after reading this book. I want this to be a book on human connection that doesn't just talk about it, but helps you *feel* more connected. Your hopes for a life released from feeling 'unlovable' are real. I know this freedom exists because I've emerged on the other side. I started my healing by reading books and talking to people, tears streaming down my face like a forgotten pot on the stove boiling over – bubbling with pain in my gut. I couldn't keep my lid on any longer. This book is designed to point an arrow at the places in your life where love and connection could flow in and fill the gaps. Then I hope it urges you to find other resources, like therapy or a coach, to build yourself back up with a more bespoke approach.

Through this book, you'll learn how to reconnect with yourself. You'll start thinking about *why* you feel a certain way when you fight with your partner, the tendrils of the argument reaching far back into your past. You'll know whom to go to when it's time to speak about your pain. You'll understand the kind of trust that's the foundation for authentic connection. I hope you'll discover ways you never thought of to reach out to stop the chill of loneliness setting into your bones. At the end of each chapter, there will be practical connection challenges that can guide you in taking action.

The aim of these exercises is to help you improve your social connectedness. Depending on where you are on your own path toward meaningful connection, however, you may find some of the tasks challenging emotionally. I'm not a therapist or a mental health specialist, but I've shared some of the tools and techniques that have helped me on my own journey from the emptiness of isolation and loneliness I used to feel to more fullness and the overflowing cup of connection I now experience most days.

I invite you to try the exercises that resonate with you, and also to keep an open mind and heart over the ones you find yourself wanting to avoid. These very exercises may hold the keys to feelings you most need to explore, or actions you most need to take. I recognize, however, that this is *your* journey, so please go at your own pace – baby steps if you need to – and with love and lots of self-compassion, and the help of a trained professional, if needs be. We all need to step beyond the pages to form relationships, and these exercises will help you do just that.

I could give you my professional bio here and tell you that I speak on stages around the world on the power of human connection. And that I've worked in front of the mic and camera for some of the world's biggest broadcasters. But as we already know, none of those things made me a master at human connection. None of those achievements healed me. In reality, your achievements won't heal you either. The media taught me to communicate, but it didn't teach me to connect. Certainly not the kind of connection I'd want to share in a book.

I think what is more important to note is the bio between the lines. As I know it is for many, a search for love and connection is the thread running throughout my entire life story. I was born in Singapore and raised in Australia to immigrant parents. My childhood was emotionally exhausting, and as soon as I could, I put space between myself and the place I was raised. I used ambition and achievement to get me out of there. Beginning with a scholarship to Switzerland at seventeen, I learnt for the first time, after living with three new families, that the shouting and walking on eggshells weren't an experience all children had.

I now have a Cavalier King Charles Spaniel called Charlie; she's the worst at saving face – ever. She fans her tail with a desperation and neediness for cuddles that stops people on the street. 'Look at her tail; it's so cute!' *She's so obvious*, they think, and point. Her whole bum moves when she wags her tail, impeding her walk. *All because she wants love and approval.* That was me. My entire way of connecting with people was impaired because I believed I was completely starved of the true connection we all need. This gave off a desperation in the way I connected with others, which was noticeable to everyone but me. This 'desperate' energy repelled the connection I wanted so badly even further. This book traces the journey into how that behavior came to be in the hope that those who see themselves in my story will find healing and connection, too.

Rather than tell you I'm a master, I wanted to open this book by telling you how I've failed deeply as a human connector. At one point or another, I may have failed in every way you can imagine, but I keep getting back up again and hope to get better at it. I hope my devotion to being better at it helps you see you can do the same. Eventually, as the chapters unfold, you'll see that 'being better' isn't optional. Through this book, you'll learn that human connection is integral to our physical and mental well-being, and there will be many studies and experts cited to support that.

I sit here now from a place of hard-won healing and a deep self-awareness that the learning never stops. I can look in the mirror and comfortably say, 'I like me.' I have beautiful friends, a purpose, a mission, and, most importantly, wonderful relationships with my remaining direct family members. Those connections are something I needed to have, to feel I could write this book from a place of resolve. This book isn't didactic, and it isn't highly prescriptive.

Just as researcher Brené Brown implies in her book *The Gifts of Imperfection*,[1] I too am not a 'how to' kind of girl. I'm not here to give you three hacks to connect with people, or tell you how to use mentalist body language techniques to control people's minds. The practical parts of this book are more observances and suggestions than they are top tips. This is also because my concerns around loneliness are ever-morphing with our changing world. Furthermore, be it from a pandemic or increased digitization, our needs for connection will change constantly. Consequently, this book was designed to walk the talk on connection, so that you would feel less alone, different, and lacking in belonging, simply in the act of reading it.

I'm Simone. *Let's connect.*

Chapter 1

SILENCE

The Secret Loneliness Epidemic

Self-connection is defined by Tim Sitt, a child and family therapist and registered social worker, as 'the process of being in touch with the worthiness and wholeness of your Self regardless of the form of experience you are having. These forms could be feelings, thoughts, expectations, beliefs, or attitudes.'[2] In a nutshell, self-connection is an awareness of your own experience. Without self-connection – effectively knowing ourselves deeply and intimately – we cannot connect well with others. Instead, we send an avatar of ourselves into the world, and people connect not with us authentically, but with behaviors born of our triggers and the lingering remnants of our trauma. In our increasingly busy and digitally distracted lives, it becomes easy to avoid the inner work of getting to know ourselves better, and avoidance means stunting our ability to connect well with others. The journey to getting to know ourselves better is a large part of what we'll deal with in this book.

The 2018 Cigna Loneliness Index surveyed 20,000 Americans and discovered that loneliness had reached 'epidemic' proportions, with almost half of participants registering as feeling 'always' or 'sometimes' alone.[3] In 2018, the UK government appointed its first Minister for Loneliness, who was charged with tackling what former Prime Minister Theresa May called the 'sad reality of modern life.' As you'll read throughout this book, a lack of human connection can lead to many different issues that you may not immediately link. Hoarding. Rage. Addiction. Depression.[4] And because of the shame associated with saying 'I'm lonely,' we've been suffering silently for a lot longer than anyone wants to admit.

The Loneliness Epidemic

In 2003, I stood watching my father give the eulogy at my Chinese grandmother's funeral. I'd just returned to Australia from studying in Switzerland for a year and, as a family, we'd made the trip to Singapore. My father had been away, a migrant in another country, for almost 20 years. His relationship with my Teochew grandmother consisted of peppered phone calls with months of silence in between, a tenuous link at best. Regardless, he had to give the eulogy because he was the eldest son in a Chinese family, and that was what was expected.

I looked up at my father, his slight paunch encased in a white polo shirt like a ripe Christmas pudding. I observed his humble demeanor, always head bowed, facing the mole on his hand that had been getting darker from time spent outside playing golf. He had only recently started taking one weekend day off each week from work at his newsagent's. He still didn't even know how to use sunscreen; that's how rarely he took a break. He would come home from golf with arms like Cadbury's Top Deck chocolate: white beneath his capped sleeves and deep brown on his forearms, then apply sunscreen, like an after-sun aloe vera treatment. Gosh, that made my sister and I giggle. My eyes became blurry as I shifted focus from his tanned forearms to his kind eyes. I heard the sound of his voice paying tribute to a grandmother I barely knew and didn't speak the same language as. I was out of my own body. A dangerous thought flashed in my mind like rogue lightning in a summer sky: *Oh my gosh – I'll have to do this for my father one day. I'll have to get up at his funeral and grieve him and say all kinds of nice things about him in the past tense, and I never want that day to come.* Little did I know, almost a year later, I'd be up there, on a pulpit, in a church, surrounded by a sea of sobs, paying premature tribute to Robert Heng.

Because at that very moment, as he was speaking, eulogizing my grandmother, a cancer was growing inside him. A cancer which, by the time it was discovered, would overwhelm his small body and kill him. It would be so painful that they would have to infuse him with morphine like I infuse my morning tea with chamomile. Fast, strong, and so pervasive that his color would change to jaundiced yellow just like the hot water in my tea. It wasn't like global warming. Here, there were no warning signs. It just happened, and our world ended. Like the cancer growing in my father, there's a cancer secretly growing in the body of the human race. It isn't COVID-19, and it isn't global warming. It is a cancer that poses huge threats to our mental and physical health and our entire way of functioning as a species. It's shrouded in shame and whispered about in communities. It befuddles TikTok-using teens with high anxiety. It exists behind keyboards and Messenger texts, between friends on social media. This secret illness is an epidemic of loneliness. The ill effects of loneliness have long been well supported by research. According to one meta-analysis, a lack of social connection heightens health risks as much as smoking 15 cigarettes a day, or having an alcohol use disorder.[5] Loneliness and social isolation are twice as harmful to physical and mental health as obesity. Even sadder is that it took a contagious virus for us to see how badly a lack of human connection affects us because, like the cancer inside my dad, loneliness has been killing us softly long before we had a clue.

Defining Human Connection

What is human connection? What is this term, so often thrown around, but seemingly intangible? It is so much easier to explain why we need it than what it is. From my conversations with digitally reared teens, I think knowing how to define human connection may be vital for Gen Z, who emerged as the loneliest of all generations in the Cigna Loneliness Index. How do we know when we're making, or are in the presence of, a genuine human connection?

We have all experienced that moment where, when we meet someone for the first time, we're on the exact same wavelength. Our opinions, morals, values, and worldviews are in sync. We see so much of ourselves in the other person that energy starts to spark off as the conversation flows and flows, and by the end of the meeting, we're inspired to hug, shake hands, or, in some way, physically touch our new friend. The connection feels right in our gut. It feels almost safe for us to disclose our vulnerabilities to this new person because we see so much of them in ourselves. I think we can agree that these connections feel distinctly different from shallow conversations shared over drinks at some business networking event. Finding new authentic connections can sometimes feel like walking around a barren desert and stumbling upon a member of your tribe that you've been stranded from!

By surveying people online, I got some incredible definitions, and they are worth featuring because of certain trends that recur. Here are some of my favorites:

- 'No one lives, or is meant to live, on their own. For me, this is powerful and humbling because it gives everyone a clue that we're all bound in a deeper sense.'

- 'Human connection is the transfer of message, thought, or emotion to another.'

- 'Human connection, to me, is the sharing or exchange of experience, either through emotions or messages.'

- 'We might not see eye to eye, but the ability to connect to something beyond ourselves is an intrinsic part of being human.'

- '[Human connection is] the experience of feeling close and connected to others. It involves feeling loved, cared for, and valued.'

- 'Human connection is about communicating with another person heart to heart. Without heart, there is no human connection!'

- 'Human connection is communication between one another.'

- '[Human connection is about] soulful conversations.'

- 'To me, human connection is when a human actively listens to understand and empathize with another human's existence, truth, and situation.'

- '[Human connection is] understanding each other.'

- 'Human connection is touch.'

- '[It's] deep interconnection of the mind, heart, and soul.'

- 'It's the bond we make with other people.'

- 'Human connection is an energy exchange between people who are paying attention to one another. It has the power to deepen the moment, inspire change, and build trust.'

- '[Human connection is] vulnerability.'

- 'It means, for me, a sense of belonging.'

- '[Human connection happens] when two people can relate to each other through their commonalities and want to continue relating to each other, despite their differences.'

- 'Human connection is showing empathy, compassion, kindness, and lifting one another despite differences. [It's] great understanding and acceptance of different views.'

- 'Human connection, to me, is our ability to share emotion, to relate to others, to rely on others, and to be relied upon by others.'

- 'To go beyond the surface and have a heart-to-heart talk. Things that matter to our soul and heart. Of what hurts, what breaks, what lifts, what matters.'

My personal definition of human connection? It is the energetic exchange we experience with another human when we're able to see, feel, and discover ourselves mirrored in them.

Wired for Connection

For me to really explain the extent to which we need human connection, we have to turn back the clock to our days in prehistoric tribes. Like most aspects of the way our brains are wired, our innate need for human connection happened when we were still in hunter-gatherer societies, running away from saber-toothed tigers. Everything about the way we operated during this time was wired to keep us safe. If we were pregnant and couldn't gather food for our family, the other tribeswomen would share their harvest with us. If we were injured and couldn't keep up with the rest of the hunt, the other tribesmen would hunt game to feed our families. And at night, when we settled down to sleep around that fire, the other tribespeople would take turns keeping watch for predators while we slept. In fact, evidence suggests that people in the past devoted significant time and scarce resources to caring for those in need. As far back as the Neanderthal era, humans have cared for their vulnerable and sick.[6] We realized there was safety in numbers, and at our core, we're still tribal creatures who crave connection. We need to have human connection, and when we're disconnected from the tribe, some really dark and scary things can start to happen.

Defining Disconnection

Interestingly, the antithesis of human connection, disconnection, is a much easier term to define. I think that could be a marker that we all have tasted disconnection: it's palpable. Dictionary.com defines disconnection as a 'lack of connection.' This is a term that will come up again and again in this book. Disconnection. Detachment. Isolation. They are all very dangerous for human beings. Johann Hari, author of *Lost Connections*, defines disconnection as being 'cut off from something we innately need but seem to have lost along the way.'[7]

Our brains imprint the feeling of that discomfort strongly for us in the hope we avoid it and stay together with our tribe at all costs.

In his book, *Social*, Matthew D. Lieberman further explains that the pain of disconnection we experience when we're cast out of the tribe has enabled our survival as a species. It's also led to our dominance and enabled humans to thrive: 'By activating the same neural circuitry that causes physical pain, our experience of social pain helps ensure the survival of our children by helping keep them close to their parents.'[8]

In a modern world, where we don't live in tribes that we can be expelled from, how do we know when we're disconnected? The red flag of disconnection can start with our sleep. Without that person keeping watch over the tribe, on your own, cast out, you'd have to rouse many times in the night to look out for predators yourself. According to Dr. Louise Hawkley from the University of Chicago, people who feel lonely will have reduced quality of sleep and experience what are called 'micro-awakenings.' Like an amputee missing a phantom leg, your brain is missing the tribe it was meant to be attached to.[9] These micro-awakenings are used to study how lonely people are. When I was serving two weeks' quarantine in Perth, Australia during the pandemic, the regular calls to my hotel room to check on my mental health would always include the question: 'How are you sleeping?' for this very reason. If you experienced less-than-optimal sleep during COVID-19, you're not alone, and disconnection could well be why.

To help us identify the different rungs of connection we need to feel fully socially connected, we can turn to the work of Bruce A. Austin at New York's Rochester Institute of Technology for help. He created a scale to measure loneliness, and states that there are three different categories of loneliness: intimate loneliness (a yearning for a person you can truly be vulnerable with), relational loneliness (a yearning to be part of a social fabric on whom you can rely), and collective loneliness (a yearning for a group that shares common interests).[10]

We'll revisit these concepts in later chapters, but here's how profound loneliness showed up in my life in 2014. After 10 years abroad with ample friends and creatives who shared my mission, I returned to Perth to care for my mom, who had become paralyzed. I had none of these three orbits of connection. It was the loneliest I've ever been. My family relationships, which were already strained, were stretched as thin as a fishing line because of Mom's condition. These stressors actually caused me memory loss. Allow me to explain:

How Loneliness Affects the Brain

During this time, I'd gotten a short-term contract at a local radio station as an announcer. I had an afternoon show and would play music and run the station's competitions. One week, I ran a contest and completely forgot that I'd just run it. I'd forget to write down the winner and which song I ran the contest after. My memory, which had always been stellar, was disappearing. I was horrified. I started wondering what was wrong with me. Did I have the same degenerative disease that gave my mom dementia at 65 and put her in a wheelchair? A disease so rare, with so little known about it, that in the private Facebook group for it, users share terrifying symptoms like: 'Does anyone else here get terrible night sweats and incontinence?'

One night a few weeks later, it all came to a head. There is a button that every radio station in the world has. They call it different things depending on what market you're in, but basically, a push of this button puts the entire radio station into automation mode while everyone at home sleeps and keeps the music playing. I'd been so unknowingly stressed by what was happening with Mom that I'd jumped in the car after my shift and driven to meet my cousin for an evening movie. All of a sudden, there was silence from the radio station as I drove along the freeway. The sun had just set, and it was dark outside; I felt and heard the gravel squelch under my tires as I pulled over to really listen closely. I felt as if every person on the road around me, sitting in their car, was jamming and toggling their radio knobs, wondering why there was silence on their favorite Perth radio station for the first time in 30 years.

DEAD AIR.

Dead air is the nightmare of radio broadcasters globally. As I moved into the emergency lane and pulled over on the side of the road, I could hear a silent, howling scream of shame from anyone who had ever taught me my craft. I scrunched my forehead, trying to remember: *Did I put the station in automation? Did I press the button?* Was this really DEAD air silence, or was this just *my* old car and *my* radio? My boss rang me shortly after and, being one of the better managers I ever had, she kindly told me it couldn't happen again. I was mortified. An engineer had dialed in remotely and put the station back on air. What was happening to me? I finally went to see my local doctor after this incident to find out what was going on with my memory. The doctor called in a psychiatrist. He said, 'Simone, do you know when people are in a car crash, they can't remember what has happened?' I replied, 'Yes, that's shock!'

'You're experiencing a little bit of that,' he said. 'All these things going through your life, your mom having a stroke, her paralysis, your family members ostracizing you, lack of friendships. These things have you in fight-or-flight mode.'

I was so confused. You see, I didn't know what stress *actually* was (much more than a word for overwork and pressure, as I was soon to discover). This was 2014; the world wasn't yet having these discussions about mental health. I didn't know that it came from a biological response.[11] I just blamed myself over and over for being an unlikable, highly strung person.

I had also ignorantly assumed moving to one of the world's most isolated capital cities, where the pace was slow and the media industry sparse, would rid me of the stress I'd experienced living as an expat in bustling cities like Dubai and Singapore. I equated slower lifestyles with less stress because I knew so little about what stress was. I never realized that my stress response systems had become altered from early on in my childhood by not having my needs for love and affection met. In short, I had no idea stress was linked to a lack of human connection.

Let me explain how a fight-or-flight response is connected to a lack of social belonging. Come back with me to the cave where we were hunter-gatherers again and imagine how, when we were separated from the tribe, our bodies experienced a fight-or-flight response to the lack of safety. Alone, we could easily be picked off by a predator, or get lost and starve. Alone, we just wouldn't survive long. Our bodies were flooded with stress hormones, like cortisol, to help us feel an urgency to find safety. In the modern context, this is OK on an incidental level: it's akin to an alarm telling you to go out and connect. The problem is now, in the way we live, more digitally connected than ever, but simultaneously chronically lonelier than ever, many of us can stay in fight-or-flight mode all the time. This means those stress hormones are flooding us constantly, damaging our immunity, and leading to many life-shortening diseases. Rigorous epidemiological studies have linked loneliness and social isolation to heart disease, cancer, depression, diabetes, and suicide.[12] As mentioned earlier, the lonely brain sleeps less and is on edge in its hypervigilance against threats and is anxious. This state of being chronically in fight-or-flight mode means that lonely people are more likely to die prematurely than those with strong social connections.

The Importance of Human Connection

There's another reason I really want to emphasize how pivotal the role human connection is in achieving the life you desire. There is a very well-known motivational theory in psychology by Abraham Maslow. Maslow's Hierarchy of Needs is illustrated in a pyramid; it lists the qualities human beings need to reach the height of their potential or 'self-actualization.'[13] Maslow created the model by studying what he believed were the top 1 percent of the college population, people he believed were thriving.

So, what has this got to do with human connection? At the bottom of the pyramid, there are our physiological needs like food, water, and shelter, followed by our safety needs like psychological safety, health, and employment. Just above that are belonging and love. Without friendships and intimate relationships, we don't move higher up the pyramid. We can't get to the next level of esteem, or reach our full potential.

Now we know that human connection and a sense of belonging can help us become our best selves. We know that we can experience a shorter life span and be stressed all the time without it. But what if the one reason we have to keep away from other humans is to protect us from a virus, and yet that same act of separation causes us to erode the very immunity we need? The irony isn't lost on me.

The Pandemic Has Caused More Loneliness

Enter the Coronavirus. No book on connection can ever be written again without a mention of the COVID-19 pandemic. The world was already suffering a loneliness epidemic, and then our ability to connect via touch was taken away from us. When I spoke to neuroscientist and clinical psychologist Dr. James Coan, he explained what happens in our biological response to disconnection:

Well, one of the things I worry most about is that, when you're overtaxed in this way, by involuntary isolation, one of the regions of the brain that is going to be fatigued or slowly disinvested in, is your prefrontal cortex, your ability to think abstractly, plan contingencies that make sense, et cetera. In effect, you get dumber, right when we should not get dumber. That's one of the things we can expect from long periods of social isolation. One of the symptoms of depression is cognitive difficulties: problems with memory, and so forth.

What COVID-19 did was push people who weren't feeling part of the tribe so close to the edge that they jumped off the proverbial cliff. In April 2020, my close friend and beloved mentor took his life in a Melbourne quarantine facility. My eyes tear up just writing this because if I could tell you how loved this person was, it's almost inconceivable he couldn't himself see his own virtues. He had left Dubai to repatriate to Australia and had left a marriage and an industry behind. Feelings of isolation can be so large and so insurmountable that many would rather be swallowed whole. Some call this darkness loneliness; some call it depression. What I know for sure is that human connection is the rope we can fling into it and allow someone we love dearly to pull themselves out. I wish I'd done that for him; I wish I'd known what was happening at that time.

The loneliness crisis we're experiencing was happening before COVID-19. I know because I was speaking about it before the pandemic, but the virus has shone a spotlight on how vital human connection is and how close we are to losing any semblance of a connected way of living. Now, if we don't do something about it, it's just killing us loudly instead of softly.

Try the following connection challenges to practice actual connection, so we don't just read and talk about it.

Reach out to those you haven't spoken to in a while

Look through your phone's most-used messaging app. Find three people who you haven't spoken to in six months or longer. Look specifically for people in your circle who may withdraw and tend to self-isolate. First, text them, wait for the text response, and then leave a voice note as a reply. If they reciprocate with a voice note, listen and connect with their voice note. Do they sound OK? Escalate the exchange using a phone call or video. Remember, the best digital connection leads to an in-person connection (more on that in Chapter 12), so create time to meet in person for a catch-up.

Pick up the phone and call someone instead of a video call

A recent study by Jeffery A. Hall, Natalie Pennington, and Amanda J. Holmstrom on connecting through technology during COVID-19 confirmed that 'Zoom fatigue' is real.[14] As a result of its ubiquity, people now associate video calls as stressful and anxiety-inducing, making them feel even lonelier. The 'old-school' phone call has thus made a return. Understand that the smile is to the voice what eye contact is to the face. So smile when on that call, so that anyone you love who might be at risk on the other end can hear your warmth expressed.

Schedule catch-ups in your calendar

It is possible, with the way we currently live, for months to go by without reaching out to people outside our intimate circle. We can make sure we look out for people at risk in our wider community and friendship circles by scheduling a monthly calendar reminder to reach out for catch-ups with people we haven't seen for a while. I do this every month.

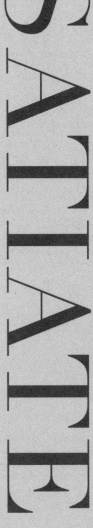

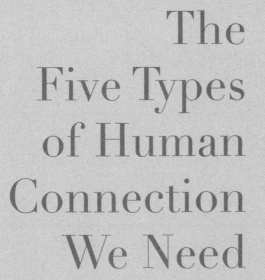

Chapter 2

SATIATE

The Five Types of Human Connection We Need

I slumped lazily at the radio panel. It was 2018, and I'd been dragging my feet through late-night shifts, while also studying the craft of speaking for seven hours during the day. The lack of belonging and bullying I'd been experiencing in my workplace had left me a shell of myself; I no longer felt excited about being in the media and I wanted to use my gift of communication to talk about things that really mattered.

We know that our words are powerful: they are energy, intention, and vibration. I'd spent almost 20 years talking about fluff. Selling other people's products and perpetuating toxic, celebrity-gossip stories. When I finally started to perceive my voice as worthy of more, that my words had value, it was already the beginning of my awakening. That evening, I felt it rising up inside me like an early morning mist. Within a few months, it would be like a revolt inside my body. Jolted from these thoughts, I realized I had to run a contest on air to give away tickets to a superhero movie.

I asked on air for people to voice-note into the station, and answer the question: 'If you could have any superpower in the world, what would it be and why?' I played the audio and heard a young woman with a Singaporean accent. She sounded unsure of herself and her voice trembled with vulnerability. She left this raw audio:

> *Hi, I'm Mei Xuan, and one superpower I'd like to have is to be able to relate to people. It's not an extraordinary superpower, but I just feel like, in the modern day, everyone is kind of cold to one another. I just want to be able to relate to a person, one on one.*

At first, I couldn't believe my ears. Had loneliness become so bad that being able to connect was considered a superpower? I believed her about the coldness – I was experiencing it in the very environment I was working in – but surely human connection wasn't a *superpower*? Mei Xuan, of course, won the competition. I gave her those movie tickets so she could go and make more friends in the process, but her voice note haunted me.

It turns out this was a harbinger of things to come, with the pandemic just a couple of years away. What was making people so lonely? Yes, there was the use of devices which, in 2018, was already increasingly disconnecting us. At the time, many people were raging with social media addictions and becoming polarized and siloed. I think the pandemic highlighted that, as much as tech connections are a great lifeline in a crisis, it's face-to-face connection we need and crave.

But I think, too, Mei Xuan and I were lonely, like many young people, because we were also confused. I didn't know how to discern what connection I needed and what connection I didn't. There's a lot of talk online from accounts and listicles, insisting that you should cut certain sorts of friends off and that we only need loyal and deep friends, but studies show healthy connection comes in many different forms, all conspiring like a beautiful ballet to make us feel socially connected.

It isn't just deep connection we need, the way those Instagram tiles would have us believe. I feel this can be one of the most damaging mythologies on connection I see proliferated online. It's making people feel lonelier because they are dropping different sorts of relationships in favor of only one type of deep connection in which they can be vulnerable. We also don't need to find every type of connection in one person, or in our romantic partner.

Let's look at the five types of connection we need, based on the studies by some of the field's best researchers.

Micro-Connections

My beautiful friend Theresa is currently mourning her father, Tim – a Hong Kong–Chinese man who, like my own father, opened his home and cooked beautiful meals for her friends at school. Theresa and I are voice-noting between Dubai, where she's based, and Singapore, where I am. She tells me her father got up every morning at 4 a.m., come rain or shine, to do Tai Chi on Streatham Common in South London, England. He would talk to and get to know dog walkers and runners early in the morning. In the wake of his death, Theresa got cards from many people in the community who had seen this old Chinese man as part of their daily lives. She received a card from a woman she had never met:

> *My name is Judy. I got your details from Maggie. Like Maggie, I met Tim on my regular morning walks around Streatham Common. I have known him for years and he became a regular presence outside the Rookery. When I missed him last year, I became concerned. I thank God for Maggie, for it's from her that I learnt the bad news that Tim had cancer. It was from her also that I've learnt of his sad death. I will always think of him as I walk past the Rookery.*

Theresa broke down in tears and said, 'It's interesting – you don't necessarily have to have people become a huge part of your life. They could just be part of your daily routine and it's human connection at its best. You connect, not through speech but rather, just on the Common, seeing each other. And after so many years, my dad's presence had so much impact.'

What we know about micro-connections, as I term them, is that they happen incidentally every single day, and they in themselves hold deep amounts of love. In her book, *Love 2.0: Creating Happiness and Health in Moments of Connection*, the incredible Barbara L. Fredrickson studies what love is and her research yields fascinating insights into what is happening in the body amid these small, seemingly innocuous, daily interactions:

> *Love, as your body defines it, isn't exclusive, not something to be reserved for your soul mate, your inner circle, your kin, or your so-called loved ones. Love's reach turns out to be far wider than we're typically coaxed to imagine... Love is that micro-moment of warmth and connection that you share with another living being.*[15]

What Maggie, Judy, and Tim all experienced on that Common was actually a form of love that blossomed into mutual care. So, if the pandemic didn't already convince you, let me say it again: we need micro-connections in our daily lives.

Every morning, when I lived in a small village in Switzerland called Eschlikon, I'd walk about six minutes to the train station to get the train to school in a larger city. On the way, I'd walk past other students, or the elderly getting their daily dose of fresh air. As we neared one another, looking me in the eye, they would say *'grüezi'* to me. I'd say this back. It literally means 'hello' in Swiss dialect. This would happen over and over again with anyone I'd meet in the village, a literal acknowledgment that you're part of the tribe. You are seen. What a wonderful gift to a foreigner who spoke Swiss very badly. Physiologically, both parties would get some mood-boosting oxytocin from making eye contact and some stress-reducing dopamine, too.

Those everyday interactions we missed so much during the pandemic have value in reducing our stress by staving off loneliness – they're not some uncanny accident. Don't take for granted the nod to your neighbor or the pat on the back to your barista when getting your morning coffee. The fact that these micro-connections have a role in making you feel more connected is supported by a study by Julianne Holt-Lunstad at Utah's Brigham Young University. She calls this type of connection 'social integration', and it's an important part of extending your life span.[16]

One of the other things I loved in Switzerland, which helps to solidify social integration, is the act of sending *'liebe grüße'.* The words literally mean 'love greetings' in German, but probably more accurately translate to 'kind regards' in English. So, if you bumped into someone you knew who had met your parents before, even 10 years earlier, it wouldn't be uncommon for them to say at the end of the interaction: 'sending kind regards to your parents.' And mark my words, you'd be expected to pass this message on! What does this practice do for us in terms of the psychology of connection? It literally increases the strength of the web of our social cohesion, reminding the person receiving the greeting that they are remembered and improving their sense of belonging. It tells the brain: *I belong to a matrix bigger than me and, therefore, I'm not alone.*

Most of the conversation in these micro-connections is what would be described as 'informational' by the Authentic Relating Practice,[17] a groundbreaking relational practice that aims to create profoundly enriching, enlivening, and nourishing relationships in all social domains of life. This 'informational' conversation is vital to our lives. It includes details that help us know where we're going, where to buy food, and how to stay safe. However, the chat here would be considered 'small talk' and be devoid of emotional content. It may often seem boring to us but it's a vital doorway for deeper bonds to build over time.

So now we know that we need micro-connections, what other types of connection are vital?

Self-Connection

As mentioned earlier, self-connection is 'the process of being in touch with the worthiness and wholeness of your Self regardless of the form of experience you are having.'[18] I find this really hard at times. Like most people, my self-worth does seem to ebb and flow based on circumstance and it's something I work really hard at improving.

You need great self-connection to connect well with others – it's actually the baseline for emotional intelligence. You can grow your self-connection at any time – it's never too late. You can do this through meditation, therapy, exercise, silence, breathwork, and your own spiritual practice. I delayed so much of the work with the relationship with myself for years by being busy, by filling my days to the brim so as not to have to sit with myself. The lesson I learnt: You can't run away from yourself. It has been in sitting in silence and listening to myself, feeling every micro-movement of my body in relation to a thought that I'm having, leaning into the discomfort of the pain this stillness may yield that I've come to understand myself better. It is with this new understanding of myself that I've been able to connect better with others. If there's one thing you can do to shift the needle in your life to move you in leaps and bounds toward the best version of you, then it's doing work around self-connection. What action plan can you mark in your calendar to begin your self-connection work? An hour aside to search for a therapist? Time to attend a meditation class? The choice is yours.

Intimate Connection

Through Bruce A. Austin's research (mentioned in Chapter 1), we know that people experience three distinct domains of loneliness.[19] I always like to take something negative and flip it, so when I'm speaking about this to audiences, I ask us to look at the research not as rungs of loneliness but as rungs of connection we need to be happy and healthy.

We need intimate connection – what you can think of as people you can truly be vulnerable with and who love you, warts and all. This is a rung of connection you really need; it trumps all others. Many people find this form of connection in their romantic partner, but I have also cultivated sets of deep friendships in all the countries I've lived in that would fall into this category.

Your intimate connections are the people who you're closest to in the whole world and who provide you with the most emotional support. According to the work of evolutionary anthropologist Robin Dunbar,[20] most people have around five close friends or family in this orbit of connection. These may often be people you live with.

What we don't want is for people to rely solely on other forms of connection without cultivating any intimate ones. Lack of intimate connection then leads to feelings of being unanchored and adrift. I think we've all felt this way, this feeling of being 'unseen' at one point or the other.

Relational Connection

This is belonging to a social fabric that you know you have access to when you need to call on it. These are deeper than micro-connections. Many people find relational connections in their family and kin. The person you can call when you need the kids babysat or to be taken to the emergency room. It's a sad fact of the way we live now that many people feel that they can't call on people that will be there for them. According to Dunbar's work, this group comprises around 15 people and these are often people who make up your identity in some way. They could include extended family.[21]

I experienced relational loneliness recently. I've been away from Perth, my hometown, for about 20 years, but I'm set to freeze my eggs there soon. In order to do so, the nurse at the clinic asked me if I had someone who could take time off work and pick me up after the procedure, as I'd be drowsy from the anesthetic. At the time this conversation took place, my cousin and best friend (who is still based there) was juggling full-time work with caring for her two young children. Without that option on the table, I sat stumped, wondering who I could ask. If we were in Singapore, no problem, but this was a place where I didn't have as active a social fabric. I later told my favorite uncle about this, and the sides of his eyes crinkled into an empathetic smile, and he said, 'Simone, of course I'll take off work to come and get you.' I burst out crying. We need people and we need this type of connection, and we need the vulnerability to ask for what we need.

Collective Connection

This category of connection is about belonging and affiliation, and knowing that you're in tune with the people around you. You don't have to be best buddies with this rung of connection, but you do have to have commonalities which thread you together.

On a recent business trip, I was stranded at LAX Airport for 11 hours. I was on my way to Canada for a speaking engagement. There, drowsing off, my neck in knots, I noticed a shivering 20-year-old a couple of seats away from me. I offered him my shawl. He said I was the only person who'd been kind to him in that airport and, over the course of our conversation, he told me his story. He'd just run away from home because he felt misunderstood by his family. He'd had a spiritual awakening of sorts, and his traditional Mexican parents thought he was possessed. He'd run from the house; he hadn't even taken his phone as his parents had called the cops on him. He started to cry.

It reminded me that we can be born into family, as you'll read in the next chapter, and feel so deeply unlike them. The need to feel that you're in tune with those around you is a type of connection family can't always provide. The need for collective connection shouldn't be underestimated. It's what drives young people to run away from home and join terrorist groups or street gangs, or just to sit by a stranger shivering at LAX on a cold night in April.

So where can you go to fill this quota of connection in your life? Research points to the incredible connective value of volunteer work and we'll address this further in a later chapter. I find my collective connection in the professional speakers' associations, where we're linked by the commonality of our rather misunderstood profession. Some people find it by joining the military. In fact, while in Austin, Texas to speak at SXSW (South by Southwest) recently, one of my Lyft drivers told me that the military saved him from gang life. He had simply transferred his profound need for collective connection from one group to another.

You can find collective connection easily in your life by looking at the hobbies and interests you have and joining groups that augment those interests. I created a public speaking online membership during the pandemic for this very reason. I wanted people to come together connected by their love for self-improvement, and the Courageous Speaking Community was born.[22]

Now that we know the kinds of connections we need, here's the key takeaway: there are different types of connections that we've been blessed with, and reducing them to just one type and forsaking the rest is making us lonelier. We should still be focusing on quality over quantity in each of these rungs, but my point is, we shouldn't cut off the friends in our cycling group because they can't empathize with our existential crisis. Nor should we expect our barista serving us coffee to collect us from the airport after a trip.

Chapter 3

VULNERABILITY

The Gifts of Loss and Grief

My phone is flashing. I've just finished hosting a radio roadshow. I put down the black handheld microphone. I'm standing in the world's biggest mall, and the fluorescent lights are blinding. The day before, I'd been in Switzerland, seeing my best friends from my time there as an exchange student. We sat at Fischer's Fritz, a stunning outdoor eatery on the banks of the Zürichsee, eating buttery Zopf bread and discussing my mom. The girls had stayed with us for three months in Australia, shortly after my dad had died, almost a decade before. They knew my mother well. They asked me how she was. I replied, for some reason tearing up: 'She's been getting worse and worse. The house is in chaos. She gets mad. I know if I get a call, it will be my turn to go back there. My sister has done enough.' My voice cracks, the way it does for so many of us when we articulate a deep fear we've long thought about, but never uttered.

Now back in Dubai, 24 hours later, the phone flashes from a private number. Somehow, my intuition tells me it's my sister. Hadn't I felt this before, this impending doom, with my father when I imagined eulogizing him? I knew this call was coming. My sister says, 'Simone, Mom's had a stroke. If I were you, I'd want to come home.'

I know this tone of voice. In our family, this is muscle memory...

The News That Takes Your Breath Away

When I was 19, I was working part time at a sports store at the local mall. My father had been in the hospital for some months, but my parents had decided to keep from us what was really going on until they had all the information. I'd like to think they were on the brink of telling us when a familiar face walked into the store. It was the nurse from the hospital treating Dad. She had a kind, well-intentioned face, like the favorite mom of all your high-school friends. We talked about the weather, and then she asked me how I was and how my father was.

'He's OK, just lashing out somewhat, which is quite out of character,' I said.

'Yes, it's like that when they have cancer,' she replied, a well-worn sadness curling her bottom lip and furrowing her brow.

I DIDN'T EVEN KNOW. I'd suspected Dad had cancer, but at that moment, I hadn't heard it from my parents' mouths. I ran off the shop floor and stood sobbing in the back room, surrounded by bricks of orange Nike shoeboxes, which I felt were caving in on me. Ninety days later, my father died. That evening, the nurse came to the house. We were told it was time. My father's hospital bed had been placed in my bedroom because it was on the ground floor of the house. My mother, sister, and I, along with my mother's brother, surrounded the thin remnants of what was left of my father. His fragility was protected in the duvet like a bird I once rescued and padded in tissues for its comfort. I clutched his hand. He was barely breathing. My mother was keening: a kind of wailing that chilled me to the bone. Her body rocked back and forth, as if in a trance. I'd only ever seen women in documentaries behaving like this after losing their babies in famine. My mother of steel was devoured without him. She melted down that evening.

My uncle shook his head repeatedly, saying, 'Robbie, don't go. Don't go.' Dad exhaled, his eyes rolled backward, and then... he was gone.

It is surreal to see someone die in front of you. When my 19-year-old self had watched movies, seeing an actor take their last breath was dramatic, but there was always an emotional distance. Something about knowing the dying person is acting sanitizes the experience. It certainly never prepared me to see the person I loved most in the world take their last breath. Those of us who have seen someone pass on are connected in that most intimate of moments.

I slept that night in my sister's room. I couldn't sleep in my room with Dad's body there. The next morning, I went to the bed he was in and looked at him with a strange detachment.

I touched his cold hand. It looked like his hand, with the mole on it I'd come to know for years. But he was thin and gray and empty. The body was just a sack of flesh. What we hear about the soul bringing the body to life is absolutely true. The soul animates. Death, in that moment, looked so final to me. There was nothing in the world that could be done to breathe life back into my father. What I saw was just the carcass, riddled with cancer. There were huge bruises on his back when we turned his body over to get him ready for the morgue. I later learnt this was postmortem lividity, where the pooling of blood after death takes on a blue-and-black mottled appearance. I'd never felt more like a child than in that moment. Why had no one prepared me for this? Why did no one protect me? It looked like he had been assaulted. Maybe, in a way, he had.

In the days that followed, I helped my sister organize the funeral program. Relatives streamed into our home. My sister held it together. My mother, sobbing constantly, was told by old Asian aunties who weren't qualified to counsel those who are grieving, 'Be strong. Don't cry.' I saw her push the natural reaction she was meant to have deep inside her. Isn't this how my dad had gotten cancer in the first place? By pushing all his trauma deep inside until, to paraphrase Louise Hay, his dis-ease became disease. I tried to do what they said because, at that time, I was conditioned by my culture to treat anyone older than me as wiser, as someone I should respect because 'they know more about life than I do.' Life has now taught me otherwise. Just because people are older doesn't mean they know more about mental wellness than you do. Pushing down my grief almost destroyed me.

We picked up my father's sisters from the airport. They had flown in from Singapore. I had to tell them Dad had passed. The first thing one of them said to my puffy-eyed face was, 'Y'all didn't pray hard enough.' As recently converted charismatic Christians, this was their belief. There was little comfort or acknowledgment of how I felt, just more disconnection. The days prepping for the funeral were so stressful, I wanted to run away. My father and I had been best friends. I didn't see the point of being at home any longer with this family I loved, but didn't really like, let alone felt I belonged to. Now I realize this internal unrest, this seeming contradiction of feelings, was the beginning of my developing my own precious voice, which would go on to become a powerful gift in my life. Your voice is powerful too. This was also actually the beginning of my self-connection. It felt just like a budding inside of me – the beginning of valuing my own opinion, away from the smothering obedience and obligation that comes with being an Asian girl in an Asian family.

The Funeral

On the day of the funeral, I watched my mother walk in front of the hearse early in the morning. We walked ahead in front of her. I'll never forget seeing her like that, crumpled over, keening like a wild animal shot in the leg, yet still somehow keeping her feet in motion. Life had hunted her. *What form of my mother*

41

will emerge after this? I wondered. *Would she become hardened and stronger, or would she soften and finally show up as the affectionate mother I longed for?*

We got into the hearse and drove to Riverton, where my father had worked at his shop for 20 years. If I close my eyes now, I can still feel the excitement of arriving there with Mom as a child after a hot summer primary-school day and seeing him behind the counter, dutifully serving someone. I'd jump up and down to show him I was there, the countertop otherwise concealing my presence. The minute his customers left, I'd run and embrace him. Sometimes he would hand me an ice-cold Coke as a treat from the mini-fridge. My father, to this day, was the most physically and verbally affectionate Chinese–Singaporean person I've ever met. In the months that followed his death, every time I had to drive past his shop, my heart would palpitate, having to reconcile the fact that he no longer existed – in his place, another man now stood behind that counter, running the shop like a mistaken alternate reality.

We entered the church, our local parish. My father had adopted Catholicism for my mom when they married. I remember him snoring away in church in the nineties, but in the months before he died, he had actually drawn a lot of comfort from the religion, and I'm happy he did. I walked behind the coffin. I'd pulled my hair around my face to avoid being judged for how I was expressing my grief. I was called up to eulogize him. To talk to people about the kind of man he was, and when I looked up, vision blurred with tears, I saw a sea of people. Literally, people streaming out into the church's grassy courtyard with Perth's autumn light unwrapping itself on their shoulders. My breath caught in my throat. How many people had shown up for this humble shopkeeper? Decades later, I'd be confronted in Singapore by a British man who claimed that it's ridiculous to think you can make a difference in this life. I didn't have the heart to shout over the restaurant music to tell him this story about my father. Maybe I felt deep inside it would have been wasted on him.

After the funeral, family members came back to our home for the wake.

One of my Dad's sisters said to us, 'Your father abandoned us when he went to Australia.'

I fled from the lounge room. I'm to show respect, regardless of how abominable the things the aunties say are. I covered my face in grief, only to bump into another aunt, this time on my mother's side. My face almost rebounded off her ample chest. I removed my hands from my face as she said, 'Why your face like that?' I touched the pimples on my cheeks I'd tried to cover with makeup. The tears must have washed it off. I wanted to justify myself, list my reasons: 'Because my dad has been dying of cancer. Because I'm stressed. Because I'm 19.'

But I didn't say anything because, from the time I was a little Asian girl growing up in an Asian house in a Western country,

I knew the rules. The rules were to disconnect from myself – my voice, my opinion – and always defer respect to my older relatives. Allow them to be as mean or prying as they liked, as critical and judgmental as they liked, as gossipy and bitchy as they liked, and say absolutely nothing. I was worn down by these people. I nodded and excused myself. It was my father's funeral, and it wasn't even safe for me to be myself.

It is conflicting because we're programmed to love our families. Some of us develop hard skin, like the outside of a snake fruit, to compensate for this lack of approval, and what feels like conditional love, paid promptly only on our obedience. Then, before we know it, we become adults. We have partners, babies, and the same people who criticized us have done their duty and are bowing out of life. Hunched over in wheelchairs and splayed out on operating tables, and we're the ones who must care for them. Take them to the toilet, pull up their diapers, and drive them to their doctors' appointments. Our culture tells us to do so. They will never say 'thank you' or 'sorry'. We owe them for the act of birthing us or simply being blood to us. We must reconnect the image of resentment with the image of them diminished, along with a loneliness born of our childhoods' 'you're inadequate' theme song, and get on with taking care of them. That's what our filial obligation says. But under this, there's rage. It's a rage of being mute when you want to fight for yourself, and it's a rage not everyone will understand. Many a boyfriend of mine could never understand it because culture is part of my skin; it's there in the almond upturn of my eyes.

You can marry into it, you can date it, but it will never be part of you by osmosis.

Human Connection Superhero

My father lived a daily practice of consistently showing up for people. Small kindnesses and acts of service, from cooking delicious meals for Asian students at nearby Murdoch University, Perth, and hosting them at Easter when they had nowhere else to go, to giving limitless tabs to elderly customers or people who were just scraping by and couldn't afford their cigarettes and scratch cards. Whenever I read articles about Teochew people being good at business, I laugh. My sister says, 'Dad was the worst at business ever.' She's right, but he knew more about human connection than most of us. He knew viscerally because he grew up dirt poor in a house full of addiction and trauma. He knew that possessions, wealth, and achievement don't ever quieten the pain. Connection does. It is the healing balm on the burn trauma leaves behind.

So you can imagine how the trauma of losing my father, in addition to not being soothed as a child, built my 'mind-reading' abilities. I'd become constantly on the alert for tragedy and wildly suspicious of bad news every time I picked up the phone to an unknown number.

So on that summer's day in 2013 in that mall in Dubai, when my phone rang and my sister's thick Aussie-accented voice – more

Julia Gillard than Kylie Minogue – said, 'Simone, if I were you, I'd want to come home now,' I knew she meant it.

I canceled my flight to my best friend's wedding in Tuscany, which I was set to attend the next day. I booked an 11-hour direct flight to Perth, and for the whole 11 hours, my heart was pounding in my chest like it would escape my flesh and hurl itself at the seat in front of me. By the time the wheels touched the tarmac at Perth's international airport, that bursting heartbeat had moved down into my stomach until it felt like a wrecking ball breaking me apart.

I went directly in my stale plane clothes to the hospital to see my mother, gray and discombobulated, in a ward with nauseating cerulean-blue walls. Her legs were spasming, and her eyes were rolling in her head like the small rotating plastic fishing game I had as a child. I'd never seen her like this before. She was in a diaper so huge it looked like she was Humpty Dumpty, with her skinny legs poking out either side. Terrifyingly, she would wear a diaper from that day onward. I knew in that moment, as I had known when my father died, that my existence would change forever.

Filial Piety

I gripped the railing at the bottom of my mother's hospital bed with white knuckles, looking on in disbelief. One of her eyes rolled again, and she hypnotically yanked her paralyzed left arm, later to be compassionately labeled by her caregivers as her 'sad arm,' over and over again across her body in desperation, to see if it could feel something. The universe spoke to me, just whispered in my ear at first, 'Simone, you have to come home now.'

I dialogued back, 'Give up my dream job for someone who was so awful to me growing up?'

When we don't have great self-connection, it's really easy to ignore this internal messaging. This process was the beginning of a cracking open of me, and now, with so much healing, I have a self-connection so strong, I can communicate what I'm feeling and how I feel about something with a level of visceral storytelling. I didn't have these tools back then.

The other thing about ignoring the universe is that the voice just gets louder. The next day, I went back to see my mother again. I was clean and disinfected and could hold her hand. Again, the whisper came, but this time much louder. It spoke clearly: 'Simone, you have to come home now.'

I spoke forcefully back to the voice in my head, matching its intensity. 'Give up everything I've built for a woman who never gave me the love I needed?' The universe was momentarily silenced. Over the next week, I went to my childhood home in between hours at the hospital. Doctors spoke in hushed tones to my sister and me that she would never walk again. I began slowly trying to appraise what my family home had morphed into. My eyes wept at the dog feces stuck to the carpets and the realization of the state that my mother had lived in during those final years. But more on that later.

I went to the bathroom where she had been found. Luckily, that day family friends had been waiting for her to show up for dinner. She had had the major stroke – the stroke that puts all sufferers of the rare disease she has in a wheelchair – in the shower. The disease takes their legs like Ursula, the sea witch in *The Little Mermaid*, until they are on their back, naked and writhing. That night I showered in that same shower, imagining my mother terrified, trembling at the bottom of it for hours in a pool of her own waste. I imagined how long she lay there horrified, with the scalding hot water she so loved to shower in, beating down on her face. The steam must have been blinding when they busted the door in and had the ambulance take her away.

As the same water traveled down my forehead, the universe howled, 'Simone, you MUST come home NOW!' It screamed so loudly that I gasped, hot water almost choking me. I had no rebuttal. The next day, I visited my mother to say goodbye before returning to Dubai to pack up my life there, my mind already made up that I'd repatriate. My mother clutched my hand with her spidery good right fist and drew me close. She spoke in a tone I'd never heard from her lips, but had wanted to my entire childhood: 'Please don't leave me like this. Please come back and take care of me.'

She had always taught us, by her behavior, that vulnerability was for the weak. Here, born of fear, it had the incredible power

48

to connect us. It also holds the key to all truly real human connection. It would go on to become a huge part of my life once I got the hang of it.

'Of course, Mama,' I said, tears streaming down my face. Within six months of packing up my life as an expat in Dubai, I was back in my hometown and totally naive about how useful I'd be in my mom's new normal. I thought my just being her daughter and being there would be enough. I wasn't totally off the mark. We now know that stroke victims become more resilient against further complications through having in-person connection than they do from medication. We also know from a famous experiment by Dr. James Coan that test subjects who held the hands of their loved ones while being electric shocked in their other hand had less activity in the pain regions of the brain than test subjects holding the hand of a nurse or caregiver.[23] In effect, this research would help me to feel more useful over a decade later when I discovered it. It was my presence as her daughter that helped cushion Mom from pain. But I wasn't aware of this at the time, and the self-loathing and purposelessness soon set in.

You see, my mom is what they call a 'two-person assist.' This means she requires two people to care for her at all times. To take her from the bed to the toilet, from the toilet to the dining room, and back again. Every time she moves, she needs two caregivers because she can't walk. I get asked by my Asia-based friends why we don't just get her a home helper, which would be normal in the Asian context where labor is brought in from the Philippines and Indonesia. Small brown women of incredible patience and fortitude leave their own homes to become live-in carers, so that the elderly don't have to be put into nursing homes and can cohabitate with their children and grandkids in multigenerational households. The backs of such caregivers the world over have been broken by trying to move fully grown men from their beds to their wheelchairs. This isn't permitted in Australia. To protect caregivers in Australia, the 'two-person assist' rule comes into play. So Mom being cared for in a nursing home means she has to wait a little longer to go to the toilet than she would if we had a home helper, but it's more humane on her caregivers this way.

In fact, they took – and still take – such good care of my mother with processes such as this, I was rendered useless. I'd sit next to her in the nursing home for five to six hours a day and watch, without being able to help. This sense of uselessness and purposelessness was also what contributed to my disconnection from the world. The only thing that saved me was watching my mother's suffering and clinging to the rationality that she was experiencing far worse than me. Her days consisted of diet desserts, reading outdated copies of *Woman's Day*, and trying to keep her eyes open for the weeknight game shows on Channel Nine. She raged against the indignity of not being allowed back into her own home without the assistance of another person and the complete demoralization of having to ring a bell and wait for someone else to come and wipe her butt on the toilet.

Forgiveness

One day, after months of watching this happen from her room floor, where I often lay on a spare duvet, I asked her caregivers if I could at least do something. I needed to be of use; that's how I was raised. I'd seen so much already, but I wasn't prepared for this. This was the day, the moment, I finally saw my mother for who she actually was. Not the person she had projected into the world, but a glimpse into who she may have been before the world embittered her. The Sandra before she was a Heng, before she was a mother, before she was a teacher. They agreed to let me help take her to the toilet. I opened the door to the bathroom.

There she stood, face pressed nose to the white-tiled wall, two meters directly in front of me. Her hands were now the ones gripping, white-knuckled, to the metal railing in this bathroom. She was standing, and I realized I hadn't seen her stand for over a year. Wearing a shirt but no trousers, her thin legs like toothpicks, muscles atrophied from being wheelchair-bound. She gripped hard to keep steady, and one caregiver swooped in to prop her up on her weak left side because she was swaying dangerously out of balance, like a bird with a broken wing. I noticed, with amusement, a printed image of George Clooney on the bathroom wall, almost touching her face. Last week it had been Prince Harry. She had asked the home to print these, so she could have something good to look at during this daily process.

But the part that broke my heart, as I glanced down again, was seeing her legs bare, blouse still on, standing there in a diaper. The sheer lack of dignity. My mother had been a tiger, authoritative and powerful. I'd never seen her this vulnerable, except for the day of my father's funeral. So here was Mom, completely disconnected from her identity. The strong replaced by the 'weak.'

I had just one job. While the caregiver propped my mother up with one arm, they would then pull her diaper down with their other hand. The other caregiver would push the commode in under her before she lost stability, and all I had to do was pull the wheelchair back and out of the bathroom to give them some space. I had one job to do, but I was horrified. I was frozen, seeing this person who had lorded power and criticism over me diminished to this: a bit-player in a macabre ballet–barre routine to undress and do a shit. This woman who had had so much influence over me that, even though I ran from her, put oceans between us, her voice would still ring in my head for every action I took. Her influence had been reduced to this. My mother caught my crumbling face of horror in the bathroom mirror. I quickly readjusted and put on my 'media face.' The eyes frozen and pupils dilated, the mouth tightly pulled upwards by force like a news anchor into a fake smile. After this incident, it would take me six years until I'd smile a full genuine smile again, the 'Duchenne smile,' where my Asian eyes crinkle sincerely at their corners.

'Are you OK, darling?' my mother asked. The 'darling' part had become new vernacular since the stroke. She was softening. 'I'm fine, Mom,' I lied, rolling the wheelchair backward into her room. I sat slumped on the edge of her bed that had been pimped out with hydraulics and an air mattress to prevent bedsores. It sighed beneath the weight of me. I sobbed. The deepest sobs. Like an animal, like I heard her cry as she walked in front of my father's hearse. This was inherited pain, transferable keening. In that moment, I saw a flash of my mother for the sum of all her experiences, and I forgave her for everything. For the fear she lorded over us, the chaotic house, and the lack of emotional support. To understand how monumental this moment was, I have to take you back to where it all began, but first...

Try the following connection challenges to practice vulnerability, the route to true connection.

What vulnerability isn't

For almost 15 years, I was paid a salary to share things on the airwaves that I may not have fully processed, or been ready to share. There was a reward loop for this – the more I shared, the more the audience was engaged and the better my show fared. The problem with this, however, was that after 15 years I became conditioned to share in a one-way manner – even in social settings. I'd be the person at your friend's dinner table telling her whole life story in a bid to connect.

I learnt something vital through this: vulnerability prior to trust being established is oversharing. It repels the exact kind of connection you yearn for because it says to the new acquaintance: 'I can't be trusted with my secrets, I'll never be respectful of yours.' It's the same feeling you get when you open up Facebook and see a post where someone rants about the intricacies of their divorce.

When I began to recalibrate my relationship with being vulnerable through my human connection research, people became less skeptical of my intentions.

Have a think: are you being present and vulnerable, or oversharing?

Eye gazing

I was recently in Laos on a semi-silent retreat where I tried eye gazing meditation for the first time. The practice of looking into the eyes of another for extended periods of time increases trust and connection, but also arouses feelings of mutual love and blurs the boundaries between ourselves and others. It's been shown that just two minutes of the practice can create feelings of affection and intimacy with someone you've only just met.

I was paired with someone on the retreat who actually annoyed me a little. This wasn't a coincidence; it was divinely intended. As the meditation went on and we sank deeper into the practice, all I could hear in my head was how beautiful this other woman was inside and out and how much I wanted the best for her. We both started crying.

I want to give you a scaled-down version of this. The vulnerability you feel upon first sitting in this connection challenge is what I want you to focus on.

Begin by choosing a person to do this with; it can be a close friend, your partner, family, or even someone at work you have issues with. You'll need a one-minute timer for this exercise, and a comfortable place to sit: a big sofa, a couple of chairs or – my favorite – a yoga mat, or soft rug on the floor. Sit cross-legged, if you're able to (or in a position that makes you feel relaxed), directly facing one another. Close your eyes and breathe in deeply through your nose, and out through your mouth, using the diaphragm to pull the breath deep into your belly – do this three times. Take your time with this. Allow the breath to truly relax you.

Start the timer for 60 seconds. Now I want you to gaze into the other person's right eye for the full minute. Notice the feelings of discomfort, maybe awkwardness and laughter, but stick with it. Now look up and set the timer again for another 60 seconds. This time I want both of you to stare into each other's left eye. See what comes up for you: do you notice flecks of color in the other person's eyes that you never noticed before? As you lean into this exercise, what feelings and thoughts start to arise as the discomfort passes? Lastly, look into each other's eyes head-on for one more minute. What feelings arise? Do you cry? Do you feel connected more than you ever have with them? What feelings come up for you?

Vulnerability allows us to feel empathy

Did you know the simple act of sharing a secret with a new acquaintance can increase the levels of oxytocin (the hormone which builds trust in relationships) in the bloodstream? This is why the emotional risk of vulnerability also connects on a physiological level.

So you can imagine the connective value when a public figure gets on the TED stage and shares a side to their story we've never heard before. I was a little girl when the Monica Lewinsky/Bill Clinton scandal was unveiling itself on TV screens in nineties' Australia. I was too young to understand fully what had happened, but I remember she was painted as a sort of villain – an 'unchaste woman' – and we never heard anything from her side to the contrary. For years, we only heard Bill Clinton's side of the story.

Decades later, Monica stands on the red dot of the TED stage and tells us that she had to shower with the bathroom door open because her mother feared she would take her own life. In this moment, Monica ceases to be any of the slurs assigned to her by the media. These preconceptions we may have had melt away and we begin to imagine what it would be like to be starting your life as a young adult and to have your name dragged through the global mud. The intimacies of your dating life are out in the world in leaked recordings. How will you date or find love again? You can't get a job because everyone knows who you are, and this could bring unwanted attention to any employer. Without love or purpose for the foreseeable future as a young 20-something, how many of us would also have been broken by such a scandal? How many of us would have had loving parents ask us to shower with the bathroom door open for fear we'd take our own lives?

It is in the power of this disclosure, this vulnerability, that we empathize with Monica. We see her more fully. How can you use your vulnerability to create more empathy in your family, workplace, and community?

Chapter 4

TRAUMA

You Love as You Were Loved

Singapore was always termed 'home' in our family. When I was about 11, I did a migrants' writing course with my mom, and I wrote a piece where I, too, called Singapore home, not computing that these were simply my parents' words, like an echo I was programmed to repeat. It wasn't 'home' to me. I'd never lived there, except for three years as a baby. I remembered nothing of it. Singapore was painted as a food-filled, fast-paced haven in my parents' nostalgia. Perth, by my reality, was dull in comparison, filled with trips to Sunday church and Saturdays in Chinese class. One day, when I was 12 and feeling brave, I asked my mother, 'If Singapore was so wonderful, why did you leave?'

Like most migrant parents, Asian or otherwise, my mother said, 'Because we wanted a better life for you children.' And then she added, 'In Singapore, when we left, all children had to take their father's race's language as their second language at school. You children would have to speak and write Mandarin, and your father only speaks dialects and Malay. I don't speak Mandarin (because my mother is Singaporean Eurasian), so you would never make it. You would have never been able to compete. We wanted you to have a chance to get into university.'

This exchange made me feel like I owed my mother the entire act of migration to a place she would rather not be. This is important for what happens in later chapters, but this deep sense of owing our parents is steeped in a Singaporean upbringing. We carry not only the pressure of academic performance but also the pressure of having been given life. It's the stuff of Asian-American stand-up comedy, but underneath the laughs is the profound understanding that you can't MESS UP. MESSING UP isn't an option, ever. And it's this pressure that started my loneliness because I was no longer connecting to my family as a child or as a human. I was connecting as a vehicle for either success or shame for myself and the whole family. This is where relational loneliness can begin for many: a feeling that, in the one place you *should* feel safe, you don't belong. There's a deep lack of acceptance within your own home, and it makes you hypervigilant all the time.

I equated this feeling of not completely belonging and not being good enough with unlovability. The way my mother parented was to give me almost enough love to motivate me to do better. My counselor calls it '80 percent love.' The thrilling 100 percent love would be doled out sparingly, based on outstanding performance as a tool to affirm. This communicated to me from a very young age that love and affection existed, but were being withheld. I eventually made the connection as a child that love, for me, was conditional and paid only upon suffocating obedience and achievement.

I still have moments now where I have to catch the way I talk to myself in the same 'tough-love' tone that my mother spoke to me. There is a part of all of us that's in automation, loving others the way we were loved. Our brains are biologically affected by how we were treated and loved as young children. How we make meaning of relationships becomes wired by these early experiences, and, should we never wake up to it, can stay with us for the rest of our lives.

In his book with Oprah, *What Happened to You?*, Dr. Bruce D. Perry sums up this idea that our ability to create healthy and genuine human connection in our lives is the direct result of the human connection we received as a child: 'The attentive, loving behaviors [of caregivers] grow the neural networks that allow us to feel love, and then act in loving ways towards others. If you are loved, you learn to love.'[24]

Together, but Alone

We've all been in a room, surrounded by people, but still felt lonely. People can be there physically, but that doesn't mean they are connecting with us. Now imagine that those same people are your family. I didn't feel it was safe to call on my direct family for a favor or help if I was in need. Any such favors would be held over my head as if on a virtual scoreboard. It made it difficult even to see my friends' families and how unconditionally loving they were. I experienced deep loneliness, and a lot of it was tied to my culture. Before we dive deeper into my childhood, I want to preface this by saying the antidote to loneliness is love and connection. The quest for my mother's love and our eventual forgiveness has been the true love story of my life. And maybe for many children, Asians in particular, the thirst for approval, validation, and love from our parents follows us for years and years and years. It's not the easiest thing to explain to people who grew up with demonstrably approving, expressive, and supportive parents, but criticism and an absence of praise defined my upbringing.

Brené Brown describes the repercussions of not having our needs for love and connection met in childhood in *The Gifts of Imperfection*: 'When those needs [are] not met, we don't function as we're meant to. We break. We fall apart. We numb. We ache. We hurt others. We get sick.'[25]

The limiting belief that I was unlovable followed me from the day I was born until I was 34 years old. It flung me into a perpetual survival mode, and this sabotaged my ability to connect with others.

Sensing We Were Different

Growing up in Australia, my strict Singaporean parents wouldn't allow us to sleep over at other people's homes. We were lucky to be allowed to go to school camps. As a result of this, I never quite realized that the shouting, the mess, the chaos, and constantly living on an emotional knife-edge was different. In my gut, I knew I was much more stressed than my friends at school. I was in a constant state of alert around my mother's moods, but I was too young to make the connection. My childhood was characterized by an unpredictable environment, with ever-changing states out of my control, and children need a consistent, nurturing environment to feel safe and thrive. My mother was dealing with her own demons, born of the rare degenerative disease she has (and of which multiple strokes are a symptom). At the time, there were no studies written about this condition. Many decades later, we now know that symptoms of depression, mood swings, migraines, and blackouts have been exhibited in sufferers as young as 18. This has been a large part of the forgiveness that underpins our relationship now. Back in 1995, however, we blamed her moodiness, disorganization, and locking herself in her room simply on the menopause.

Unpredictability in a primary caregiver, even from infancy, deeply affects how a child creates their worldview. I long held a narrative that people were unpredictable and not to be wholly trusted based not only on my mother's mood swings but also the turbulent relationships and gossip that characterized some of my extended family's relationships. Living with this distress put me permanently out of balance. To this day, my internal blueprint craves a rollercoaster journey through life, rather than a smooth ride, and I'm always having to keep this in check.

My mother and father were married at 21 and 24 and then tried to conceive babies for 13 years. As a result of the decade-and-a-half wait, I was born when my mother was in her late 30s. Normal for the era we live in now, but very late compared to her peers. I always felt my parents couldn't keep up because they were older than my friends' parents by over a decade. The house was so disorganized, and the sheer chaos of being in that house felt terrifying to me as a child. There was no routine. Lights were broken and not fixed for years. No fresh fruit or vegetables in the fridge. My mother was the biggest fan of canned food; I didn't even know it wasn't good for children until a friend at school told me. Toast and canned soup were her favorite things to feed us on weekends. I'd often eat cake for breakfast if an aunty had dropped some off. It was usually the only non-expired food in the fridge.

Our clothes were washed on an *ad hoc* basis. Once I got old enough, I learnt to use the hand washbasin when I'd run out of fresh underwear because I was scared of putting the wrong items in the washing machine and breaking something that would cause me to be shouted at for days. The disorganization and lack of clocks that worked in those analog days meant my parents could never manage their time. There was always shouting before needing to leave for any outings. We had pets that my mom treated terribly, as if the dogs were there to be cheap guards for her house versus being creatures to be cared for. Once, I went back home for a trip when I was living in Dubai and found her Doberman in the backyard with rashes and flies gnawing off the flesh around his anus. She hadn't washed him for years. I wanted to hold him, but he was skittish from neglect. I looked into his sad eyes and recognized my own as a child.

Yet when it came to saving face, my parents were fantastic. My mom would make us clean the house all day if we were having people over. She would bring out the best table settings. My father would go to Fremantle Markets and buy the most succulent squid and prawns. 'Four times the size of those in Singapore!' he would proclaim, still impressed after a decade in Australia. I would relish these gatherings because I'd know we would enjoy reduced shouting from Mom in front of other people and have leftover real, tasty food in the fridge for a few days. I vowed when I grew up that I'd never live like this.

In addition to being a generation apart from my peers' parents, mine were also a culture apart. By the time I was a teenager, my mother was going through menopause. She'd had a full hysterectomy. I remember her being mad at us all the time. I felt I was a total inconvenience. Her behavior was incongruous to me because it didn't match my father's stories about how long they tried for babies. Finally, they found a doctor to treat her endometriosis, and my sister was born; I was an added bonus two years later.

One evening when I was nine, the *Grease* movies were back-to-back on TV in one of their marathon promotions. One of the lead actors, Jeff Conway, played the villain Kenickie and had the same deep acne scars along his face as Mom. My observation as a child was as innocent as running your hand through sand at the beach and noticing texture. I just connected those same scars on Kenickie's face to the ones I saw on her. I ran to her as she was seated on the couch. She never hugged us; I longed to be held by my mother. I raised my hand to try to touch her cheek, and she grabbed my hand before I could. I said to her, 'Mommy, you have the same skin as Kenickie. What is this?'

She pushed me off her and got off the couch. She was enraged. I was petrified when she would get like this. I felt stupid and awash with shame that I'd even tried to touch her. She retorted, 'Yes, you children destroyed my face.'

I had no idea what this meant and was too scared to ask. Many years later, I finally asked my father, and he replied, 'Your mom had to take some very crude hormone medication to conceive, and that's how her skin became like that.'

I felt I owed my mother her skin, her beauty, her migration. I carried this burden with me for my entire childhood like a sack of bricks on my back, and it cornered me into my decision to leave Dubai and return to be with her in 2014.

Top Marks in the Class

As I grew older, the dysfunction with which I learnt to relate to my mother was hardwired into me. I had a deep fear of her and had developed a trauma-altered stress response. Things that my peers at school found trivial weighed heavy on me with pressure. I remember losing three marks on an English paper in high school. Twenty-two out of twenty-five. I was proud of it; it was the top grade in the class. After school, I announced it buoyantly to my mom, sweat still in the small of my back from walking my huge textbooks home in the 35-degree heat.

'I was top of the class for this paper, Mom,' I announced, waving it in sweaty palms.

The words 'top of the class' were like an addictive *Daily Mail* headline to her. The kind of statement that would stimulate a jolt from her on the couch, particularly if someone else's child was 'top of something.' My voice was trembling, trying to conceal the straining for her approval. My heart was palpitating; hoping that she would be in a good mood today to hear this news. Yearning, as always, that she would see me fully. My mother looked at the score scrawled in red pen with a circle around it at the top of the page and, without smiling, shook her head. 'That score makes top of the class.' She almost spat the words with disgust.

She tutted, in the same way most of the Asian migrant mothers would, at the complete indulgence of the Australian school system. As if they were owed better for the trouble of migrating. That the system was building slovenly, lazy children. As if they didn't already know they had come to a country where everyone, and I mean everyone, who wants in gets into university. Isn't that why they chose Australia?

This was followed by, 'Go back into class and ask Mrs. M. where you lost the three marks.'

Her tone let me know she meant it.

I was mortified. What could be less cool and more foreign to my Australian teacher than having to do this? In years to come, I'd understand that what my mother was actually trying to give me was a profound gift. She felt she was teaching me to fight for myself in the world. To not take less than I deserved, and to avoid the mediocrity from setting into my bones like wood rot. Being average, I was led to believe, was contagious. I've since learnt, however, that always needing to fight for yourself makes life a fight, and it's exhausting. I see that now in my mother's sunken cheeks and paralyzed face, the face of a person for whom life was about grasping to control. Life finally taught her that it wouldn't be tamed when it took my father. Life betrayed her by incentivizing her daughter to always live far away. I look at her now with love, but I'm glad I unplugged and deprogrammed.

Confronting Authority

Friday – it was a balmy three o'clock in the afternoon. Golden Perth sun streamed into the classroom, threatening to expose my hot cheeks and shame. I could hear the sounds of other kids giggling, chatting excitedly about their weekend. That's how I saw a lot of my childhood: me being forced to do something inside while other kids, white kids, were outside having what seemed to be deep, bottomless blue swimming pools of fun.

On school holidays, I'd help my dad serve customers at his shop and tiptoe enough to crane my neck over the kiosk counter and see other kids riding the mall's mechanical animal ride and licking ice cream drips off chubby, sweaty hands. Laughing. I was envious. Deep, emerald, crystallized envy. And yet, working and being diligent when others weren't became part of me. Even as I write this, it's Sunday morning in Singapore, and while I can hear people on the street laughing with their families, I'm still inside working. It isn't strange to me. It is part of me, like the warm remnant of heat off a parent's hug I rarely felt. I work because it reminds me of them; it's all I have left of them.

My hands trembled with rage as I pushed forward the paper to Mrs. M., the paper once pushed with decisive pride to my mother, now quivering from those same hands like sails on a boat within a furious sea. I felt enraged that Mom was putting me up to this and even more enraged that I was so programmed to obey. I knew that night when she came home dog-tired from work, too tired even to cook or buy us food to eat, that she would NEVER forget to ask about my education. EVER. I opened my mouth to speak and said, 'Mrs. M., my mom wants me to ask where I've missed out on these three marks and why.'

Mrs. M., a kind, patient woman, had children of her own in our school. She was a mother. In my maladapted narrative of human connection, which I explained earlier, I felt sure she was just sick of Asian parents and Asian migrant kids keeping her behind after work because of their own cultural hang-ups. Haggling for grades must have seemed distant and foreign to her, not to mention undermining her authority. As she spoke, like many moments you'll hear about in this book, my mind left my body. Her lips moved, but I heard nothing but the shame of it all ringing tinny in my ears, my being deprived of fun, the chaos and shouting of insults in my house, the lack of non-expired food in the fridge when I wanted something to eat while studying for grades that I felt my existence depended on – all of it made tears roll down my face. I felt tired. I was 14, yet I was emotionally exhausted.

'Yes, and now I see we have the tears again,' said Mrs. M. My brain returned to my body. I snapped back into reality.

I'll never forget that line for as long as I live. That I must have had conversations with her before where I broke under the pressure of what was expected of me. To me, the skepticism on her tongue meant she couldn't possibly understand me, and it just affirmed the lack of trust in people that I'd already been forming. She couldn't imagine what it was like to live in my house. My house, with its lack of psychological safety. A house so large but so empty of the things kids need. *Mrs. M. has no idea*, I thought. *She has kids, she deals with hundreds of kids, and she thinks this is a put-on melodrama? She thinks my family is what my mother makes us project. Churchgoing, award-winning, respectful, don't-ask-for-anything immigrants, and how dare I now ask for this!* I vowed never to show vulnerability again, and I didn't for 22 years. In its place, I put ambition because ambition would put oceans between me and this place, where no one understood me.

First Love

In Dubai at 24, I fell head over heels for the kindest man I've ever met. He loved me with a ferocity I've since never known, a ferocity we feel when we fall for the first time. Things were great until I found myself picking fights and pointing out flaws. I couldn't let us slip into calm. It had to be the rollercoaster of feelings; it had to be a tugging and wrestling for even more love, as if I needed 120 percent to make up for the 80 percent I'd experienced my whole childhood. It almost broke him. Now he was the exhausted one. I had to be in fight-or-flight for anything to be real, to feel anything. This is the stamp of trauma on our psyche, like a cattle brand on your heart. This is how it sabotages your human connections. You will relive the conditions of your childhood home in your relationships with other people, in the workplaces you choose, and the friendships you stay in, until you see the pattern clearly and seek help.

There was mercy in that relationship ending; I'd have destroyed him over time. He deserved and got better from someone else, and I dragged my feet into therapy a decade later to ask tepidly,

'Is love always meant to feel like this?' The answer was 'No,' and that's how my journey toward healing began.

Juxtaposition

Remember I mentioned I had to move 4,000 kilometers away to confirm that the way I grew up was different from that of my peers? I'd passed off most crazy things as 'just being an immigrant kid', rather than acknowledging my hunch that the chronic stress was damaging me. At 17, I secured an exchange to study in Switzerland. Over the course of a year, I lived with three different families. Each family was delightful in their own way. My first family was mixed Swiss-Argentinian, and they are literally the most generous people I've ever met in my entire life. The children in this family loved each other deeply and truly treated me as if I was their own sibling. There was never fighting, shouting, or raised voices. Both my host parents worked, and the house was still spotless. My mother had always said our house was messy because she had to work so hard, but here was evidence that everyone could work *and* wash clothes *and* buy food for their children. We also had a cleaning lady once a week growing up, and there were still no fresh groceries on the regular. The penny started dropping.

My second host family barely spoke any English. Their kids had long grown up and, in their retirement, they were kind enough to house an exchange student. This was the first time in my life that a mother made me a packed lunch with so much care that

I wanted to cry. Vreni would make me Swiss Bircher muesli and separate the grated apple for me so that when I went to school, I could mix it in, and it would still be nice and crunchy. I'd never experienced mothering like this. Mom, at the height of her moods, would give us a can of Campbell's soup to take to school, still condensed, and ask me to tell the lunch lady to open it, warm it up, and mix it in water. Some lunchtimes, by the time I got to the front of the line on a cold winter's day, the bell would ring, and I wouldn't have time to eat, let alone get the can open. My dad would later start allowing me to take coins from his coin bowl so I could buy some proper food to last me through the day. Sometimes I wonder how smart I could have been with the right fuel in my little belly.

The last host family I'm actually so close to that I consider my host mother to be a second mother to me. She had a lot of the best qualities of my biological mother. I found comfort in her directness because I always knew where I stood with her – an important thing as a foreign student living in the home of people who speak a language you don't yet fully understand. As is the tradition of many Swiss *hausfraus*, Irene can cook most people under the table. In all three of the homes I stayed in, the energy was calm, the voices low, and the words supportive. It was this experience, living full time with three very different families in one year, all of whom were consistently loving, that started me suspecting that maybe I wasn't so loathsome, unworthy, and unlovable. Maybe something bigger was at play.

It was also always amazing to me when I moved back to Singapore for work and spoke about these experiences on social media that I'd receive message after message saying this is how many Singaporean adults my age still feel about their upbringing. There is immense pain carried by a child when they swap their humanity for being a vehicle of shame or success for their family, and are constantly criticized for every attempt to bring them pride. This is the root of relational loneliness for us. This feeling that made me feel so bad about myself as a child was experienced by not just me, an Asian kid in Australia, but by Asian kids in Asia. And from the hundreds of conversations I've had about it, I think the relational loneliness we experience comes down to one thing: a lack of expression of pride.

Now don't get me wrong, I'm a proud Asian woman, but I'm also an advocate for healthy human connection. So, if a child constantly hears that they aren't good enough, that they are underperforming, or, most crushingly, that they are compared to others, that they should be more like their siblings, cousins, or some kid at school with high scores, that's traumatizing to the fragile sense of self they are developing. If, in addition to this, they don't get any positive affirmation, it can lead to a lifetime of chasing validation. And chasing love, approval, and validation deeply inhibits the formation of authentic adult relationships.[26]

We already know that you can't become great at connecting with others when you don't have a great connection with yourself. It wasn't until I had the vernacular to say my childhood was traumatic; it wasn't until the dust of where I came from settled; it wasn't until I healed after arduous hours in therapy and study that I was truly able to be a decent human connector. To be compassionate and present, to forgive and serve others, this is when my cup 'runneth over', when the fog of trauma lifted. Of course, I still fail at it at times, but I'm always improving. Looking my childhood in the face, calling out the truth of what it was, I was then able to forgive my mother comprehensively and be at peace with my childhood. Here are some self-connection challenges that will help you connect better with yourself, others, and your childhood:

Connect with your childhood memories

Self-connection is the key to connecting with others. A great place to start the process of knowing ourselves better can be knowing where we came from. Gently, think back to your childhood. Are there any tenuous existing relationships that may need reconnecting? Was there trauma not spoken about, or swept under the rug that you've been avoiding sitting with and processing?

Reach out for healing

Reach out to a sibling or parent and ask them about things that may have been haunting you. Remember there are multiple truths to any viewpoint. For example, the accounts of Australia being colonized by the British will be wildly different depending on whether you speak to an Indigenous Australian or a colonizer. However, like it or not, both of these contradicting accounts exist in history. Using this as a metaphor, even if a sibling, parent, or relative doesn't feel the same way about your recollection of an event, it doesn't mean your feelings and version of the event aren't valid.

If you're aware there's some trauma already, like loss in your direct family, connect with a trusted counselor or therapist in your area.

Chapter 5

The
Relationship
Between
Human
Connection
and
Addiction

In 2014, after I returned to Perth to help with my mom's transition to the nursing home, she got an infection. I'd been called by the nursing home staff and rushed into her room only to see her face red and swollen. At the foot of her bed towered a woman, who I'll call Rhonda. Rhonda had Alzheimer's and cancer; she has since passed. She was convinced my mother was her late husband. As I walked in, Rhonda had just slipped out of lucidity and become aggressive.

My mom, unpredictable and sassy, didn't seem frightened at all. Rhonda was almost six feet tall and fully mobile. *If she's this tall now, how tall was she before she started shrinking?* I thought. Nursing homes are full of people shrinking. My mother is tiny and stuck in a bed. Next to Rhonda she looked like a fragile lone quail's egg cocooned in a nest of blankets. Rhonda gripped the end of the bed and decisively turned her head to me, sneering at my presence, nostrils flared, like a scene from *Jurassic Park* when a T-Rex smells a human.

'Who are you?' she snarled.

'I'm Simone, Sandra's daughter. Why are you in Mom's room?'
I secretly press the call button behind my leg. Here's the thing
about dementia: in that moment, Rhonda was, in her mind,
possibly her 35-year-old self. She had an energy and posture
that went back in time, and her forcefulness could have been
that not of a 70-year-old but someone my age. I could have been
flung across the room. This is the power of the mind over the
body. One of the things I love the most about my mom's nursing
home is that residents who physically can walk are free to do so;
you just run the risk of them sometimes walking unannounced
into the wrong room that they think is rightfully theirs. This day,
it was even more tenuous because Rhonda also thought Mom
was her long-dead husband.

'You're not her daughter. That's my husband,' she said, red-faced.

'Look, Rhonda, Mom's sick. I need to take care of her.' My mom
looked on, amused.

'She's not your mother. What are the names of our children?'
she asked us.

'Gerald, Sally, and Andrew,' my mother replied, satisfied. She'd
tapped into something that I was ignorant of at the time. My
mother had learnt that the best way to handle people with
dementia was not to challenge their belief when they were
agitated, but to go with it. I wondered for a moment where
she had learnt this nuance. Rhonda was her closest friend and
neighbor in the room next door. Mom had already had two new

neighbors since then. I thought, *This is how people learn the ropes in prison quickly to survive.* I was proud of my mom that even with her ill, broken brain, she could still adapt and learn. The irony of this now is that her own mind has deteriorated, so we placate her the same way she once did Rhonda. We pretend my dad is still alive, that he's just gone on holiday instead of gone into the ground.

At this point, Rhonda started coming at me with her hand raised, and just before the moment of impact, one of Mom's incredible caregivers swooped into the room. Rhonda paused, baffled. The caregiver grabbed her arm and moved her gently to the next room. I can still picture Rhonda's silhouette crumpling in the door-frame. She was lucid again, remorseful, and apologetic for not remembering what she'd done. She folded her six-foot frame to what seemed half her height, and was led by the arm to the door, her forearm skin patched like mortadella from years baking under the Australian sun. She's guided by the plump, brown hand of her caregiver. Skin made in Manila, brown skin that sought a better life in Australia, only to wipe the butts of the elderly daily for a tiny wage and never to complain. Make it look easy. Do it with grace. Take abuse. These people are walking saints.

Mom's caregiver returned to tell me: 'Your mother has an infection, for sure. Her fever is very high, but it's a Friday evening, and the doctor can't come until Monday. So, you can wait until then or call an ambulance and take your mom to the emergency room at the hospital now to see a doctor.'

The same hospital where it all began a year or so earlier when I'd walked in, fresh from that plane from Dubai, to see my mom gray-skinned and terrified. She looked rather terrified again in that moment. I asked her if she wanted to go to emergency and noticed the deep rings around her watery green eyes. Her face was totally swollen red in contrast.

I'm still trying to wrack my brain now for how I got to the hospital – if I rode in the back with her, or took my car, or called a cab and followed along. The fact that I can't remember is a sign of the deep survival mode I must have been in. What I do remember is that I had good reason to be in fight-or-flight because what found us in that hospital on a Friday evening was worth fretting over, and it wasn't actually my mother that I needed to worry about.

Scratching on Plexiglass

The waiting room, filled with screaming kids with minor injuries from skateboarding accidents and the like, cleared by 10 p.m. The screams and howls were now from adults. Clerks sat behind Plexiglass sheets to protect them. Addicts. Parched skin the texture of a chewed cigarette, eyes hollow, and wiry fingers scratching. So much scratching, on skin and clothes and plastic waiting-room chairs. I clutched Mom's hand tight at that moment, realizing why she had been so strict my entire childhood. She was protecting us from a subculture our interlocked ethnic conservative Catholic community had rarely seen. I was 30, but still so naive. Then the scratching on the Plexiglass turned to a banging. A pregnant woman howled. Her partner, who was wearing a crushed leather jacket and worn cap, brought her forward and begged; they begged for something. They were refused. He became angry. She howled again. I closed my eyes, and for the first time, I felt real fear, not from within my own family but from an external threat. I also felt deep fear because this was just another moment where I realized my mother and I had swapped roles. She'd been shrunk into my daughter, and I'd become her mother. I was mother to a 68-year-old in diapers.

We were admitted and put into a small, dark room. What looked like a white shower curtain formed the only barrier between us and the people outside. The curtain came only halfway up, so I could see the shadows dancing every time someone walked past. My mom was sliding out of her wheelchair now. It was five hours past her bedtime. I put the brakes on her chair, squatted at the knees, and in a chest-touching embrace, dragged her back into the chair. I thought about how many years I wished for that hug as a child and the macabre way in which I got what I wished for so ardently. I held her hand as she slept, my chin resting on the top of the plastic chair and the back of the chair between my legs. This looked like a far more comfortable position in music videos than in reality. I remember the plastic cutting into my thighs as I winced at the sound of the screams.

Friday evening in emergency in that hospital was full of people suffering. Not in the gentle way people slip away in nursing homes, like candle wax silently melting, but in a violent, excruciating tug-of-war. I wondered how Mom could sleep through it, but thought that maybe the nurses had given her sleep meds before we left. I could hear the rustling of a scuffle in the cubicle next door. The in-between-dream-and-awake stage yielding phrases like, 'It's OK, you'll be OK' from the medical staff. Intoxicated, indecipherable, slurred speech replying. The energy was dark and unyielding, and the way my mother was cared for there was very different from the tenderness given when she had been upstairs in the stroke unit the year before.

I look back and see the young Asian doctor, Malaysian or Singaporean, frantically checking my mom's vitals. Peeling back her diaper quickly to check for a urinary tract infection, rustling it open with haste, the way kids open Happy Meal boxes from McDonald's. Impatient fingers frantic because it was obvious there were bigger things going on that evening in emergency.

Finally, as the sun came up, we were released. I was relieved when it was over; we'd made it through the night. I often wondered what the point was. Essentially, we'd just had our own horrific slumber party. She was made to sleep in a chair, and so was I. She was given some meds, but really there wasn't much change. Then I realized this was our first overnight evening together since I was a kid. Is that what my mom had wanted all along?

A Lack of Connection Leads to Addiction

What haunts me are the sounds of the screams and my horrific ignorance. My borderline judgment of those suffering because their affliction – addiction – is so much closer to me and to all of us than we'd like to think. Addiction expert Dr. Gabor Maté believes that we're all not as distant from addicts as we perceive. That there are so many 'behavioral addictions' fostered in our current culture, from workaholism to social media addiction; that we can learn a lot from the treatment of addicts on how to heal our own behaviors. Most important to the work in this book, he believes that at the root of the problem is a disconnection. This could be abuse, trauma, or just a 'hurt.'[27]

In their book *What Happened to You?*, both Dr. Bruce D. Perry and Oprah elaborate on this idea.[28] They state that a lack of human connection as early as infancy, when a child cries for food or to have their diaper changed and their primary caregiver doesn't respond, can cause the infant to become out of balance and develop chronic distress. The child forms the worldview that people are not safe or supportive because their basic needs weren't met. Ideally, an infant's needs should be soothed in a loving, attentive, consistent environment. This then helps the child associate human connection with reward. Childhood trauma links so powerfully to human connection and addiction because the child that isn't soothed of their distress goes into chronic fight-or-flight mode; they then become particularly vulnerable to addiction. The addictive substances or behaviors are used to regulate their trauma-altered stress response and provide respite from this chronic distress. This is what makes addictions so hard to shake because the relief is sometimes the first time an individual has felt calm and balanced in their entire existence, and that yearning for peace and calm keeps pulling them back in. Individuals who have their needs for human connection met in early childhood can more easily resist being pulled into an addictive behavior because that chronic distress isn't there, constantly pleading to be calmed.

Love, Addiction, and the Search for Connection

Many years after my fearful experience with my mom in the basement of that hospital, I learnt in therapy that a large part of the source of my personal hurt and pain stemmed simply from feeling unlovable. I was a love addict: someone in constant search for connection, with a deep thirst for love and approval. In each new person I met, I didn't see a human: I saw a vessel for possible validation and adoration, which I equated with being loved for a fleeting moment. This is why so many personalities like mine choose occupations in the public eye – to soothe the pain of unlovability through the perceived love fame appears to bring. Yet fame is the opposite of connection. Even at my low levels of notoriety, I've found that fame is people connecting with an avatar of you that you construct, versus who you actually are.

This is hard for me to write. Human connection was something I deeply craved, but as I mentioned earlier, the act of chasing after it repelled it further. Learning to connect with myself and then connecting better with others comprised a large part of my healing. Of course, there are many moments I still get triggered, but I've stopped irrationally trying to chase love and authentic connection from everyone. I'm at peace with the fact that not everyone is for everyone. Finding genuine human connection, deep love, and acceptance among my intimate relationships, family, and friends, and a group with a collective purpose was the direct route to my healing (and of course, that journey is still ongoing). Obliterating all three orbits of loneliness – intimate, relational, and collective – was the answer. It has taken, and still takes, a lot of work to align those three orbits of connection, but it's my hope that through this book's connection challenges, I'll be able to encourage you into starting on that same journey.

How Connection Heals

So how do we heal? On a video conference with me, Helen, a 39-year-old Singaporean woman who calls herself an 'alcoholic in recovery', says she reminds herself to remain devoted to the process of healing, that she isn't fixed and perfect yet. She's been in active recovery for eight years and began drinking at age eight. From her first sip, she always wanted more: 'It's a physical dependency and also a mental obsession, so it's a mind-and-body thing that affects me. Alcohol was my mother, my father, my lover, my everything – up until the point it failed me.'

Prior to her second year of sobriety, Helen says she 'acted like an orphan,' like she didn't have a family. She recently made amends with her mother, from whom she was estranged for 16 years.

Human connection has been a key tool in her healing, functioning in three ways. First, through self-connection. The moment Helen realized alcohol no longer served to give her the effect she wanted, that her body could literally no longer keep it down, was the moment she knew she had to let it go. Second, recovery groups ended her collective loneliness by connecting her to a tribe with a common understanding:

> I had never identified with a group of people or friends before. My best friend helped me understand what the 12-step recovery group did for me when she said, 'Helen, thank God you finally found a group of people who understand you in a way that we never could.' I identified like-minded people in meetings who shared the same affliction. People who were laughing through darkness, and understood that darkness. I felt connected.

Lastly, part of Helen's recovery was relearning to connect with others again, getting to know her true self completely apart from her addictive behaviors. From here, she began to make amends in the relationships that she'd lost through her addiction:

I had to learn to crawl again. Open a letter without drinking.
How to answer the phone without drinking. How to connect to
someone outside of a recovery room. How to even connect with
my own husband while not drinking. I had to work to be the
best version of myself, to be the best version for them. A better
wife, a better friend, a better daughter, a better sister. The closer
I am connected to something bigger than me – that includes
being of service, support, and helping others – the further away
I am from a drink.

If, like me and so many others, you've felt the burn of unlovability and you suspect your needs for support, love, and connection weren't met in childhood, it's absolutely not too late to heal addictive behaviors. It starts by building strong orbits of people around you who care for you authentically, spend time with you, and support you. This is the first step to moving from an unhealthy soothing of your distress. In the words of Dr. Bruce D. Perry: 'Connectedness counters the pull of addictive behaviors. It is the key.'[29]

Addict or not, here's what we can learn from the relationship between human connection and addiction:

Share your pain

Self-connection, that process of 'connecting with the worthiness and wholeness of your Self,' as Tim Sitt defines it, is key.[30] I was unaware for decades that I had a love addiction, and it was deeply affecting how I connected with others. When painful feelings arise, are there parts of your life you gloss over, choosing to push down and not process, favoring other behaviors? If so, how can you slowly lean into remembering, processing, and maybe eventually sharing those moments with a trusted intimate connection with whom you can truly be vulnerable

Think about your family history

Healthy family relationships are vital. This is where we first learn how to connect. Were there feelings of not belonging and unlovability? Were your needs met for attention, support, and basic resources? I know it's daunting, but how can you reach out and make amends for your part in the disconnection of those relationships?

Serve others

As Helen mentioned, her life got better when she could be of service and support to others. This is one of the most beneficial elements of addiction support groups. Are there people who are at risk, or are there addicts in your family or close circle? If you feel you're in a strong enough place to do so, how could you support them in their recovery? We'll go even further to talk about the immense connective benefits of being of service in Chapter 11.

Chapter 6

ATROPHY

The Effect of
Isolation on
How We
Connect

When I repatriated to be with Mom after her stroke, as the second punch in the face that happens when people we love become incapacitated, I had to take care of all the stuff that she accumulated in her life and left behind.

And for me, because my father passed away too, that was 70 years of their belongings, 35 years of each of their things. My mother has hoarding disorder. And before you laugh at that, hoarding is to me, someone who experienced it at ground zero, one of the worst symptoms of loneliness. This is because it starts with loneliness and then leads to more loneliness, simply as the result of how the hoard physically isolates the hoarder. Hoarding, I've learnt, is screaming out because you're lonely, but with possessions. It was only in 2013 that hoarding disorder was included in the *Diagnostic and Statistical Manual of Mental Disorders (DSM-5)*.[31] But while they were busy classifying it, I was buried nose-deep, cleaning it. We knew so little about it. The vast majority of people with hoarding disorder (92 percent) also have another psychiatric disorder. Dementia and organic brain syndromes are very common among people with the condition.

So yes, it's an actual mental disorder like depression, but it still isn't seen that way in the eyes of most people. It's still shrouded in shame and ridicule.[32] My hope is that what you read next in this chapter will help to destigmatize it.

Sculptures of Loss

In 2014, after Mom became ill and her memory became more patchy, I began asking aunts and uncles to help me learn more about who my parents were before they had children. One aunt had said my mother was extremely house proud, wrapping bricks with the same fabric as the curtains to create some sort of DIY matching doorstops – hey, it was the eighties! Despite my personal aversion to matchy-matchiness, this story sounded like the mother I knew up until the age of 10. A mother who would book us into plaster painting and flower arrangement classes on school holidays. Hoarding disorder, I then realized, was a coping mechanism of hers to the trauma of losing so much. It wasn't her personality.

The cleanup of your parents' things isn't something you can outsource. You can uncover some horrible secrets that no one else outside of your family should see. I have a friend who found presents that her father had wrapped for his mistress. I have another who found letters her mother had written to the Vatican, begging for a divorce from her father. My disconnection from the world started because, unlike when my father died or people pass away, and the community understands and rallies round you to help – dropping off hot casseroles and groceries – hoarding disorder is steeped in mystery. People don't understand it. It's not something about which I can say, 'Hey, can you please come and help support me cleaning my mother's 35-year accumulation of trash?' The hoarding atrophied my social skills because I quit my job again, this time on the radio in Australia. And from 9:00 a.m. to 5:00 p.m. every day for six months, I cleaned. I stopped seeing people, I stopped reaching out to people. Even my sister wanted nothing to do with it. Sorting the hoard alone became my life. I lay every night exhausted by the process of sifting through stuff and dreading getting up the next day with barely any sleep to start cleaning again. Through the cleaning, I could literally track my mother's disconnection with the world through possessions. What I learnt is etched in my memory forever. Where I once saw a pile of clothes, I now see sculptures of loss. Tributes to trauma.

I found enough rubber bands to melt into a basketball, quilting magazine after quilting magazine after quilting magazine. And then the feces of those Maltese terriers stuck to the carpet, turning white, that my mother had piled more things over. Large, yellow, dog-pee stains on the antique Chinese carpets she had migrated to Australia with – once so precious to her that, as children, we weren't even allowed to have drinks in our hands when stepping over them. To allow things to become like this, I knew there must have been a cracking of the mind, a letting go completely of any standard that connected her to social norms.

We had a nine-bedroom family home as an antidote to small-apartment living in Singapore. My parents had built this huge, 1980s-style colossus with glass blocks, like something out of *Scarface*. The house had high ceilings and was painted completely in white. Even a simple child's birthday party would leave horrifying powdered chocolate fingerprints from cupcakes on every banister. I'd proudly, and without thinking it a slight, call it 'the messy mansion' to my visiting Singaporean relatives who 'oohed' and 'ahhed' at its basketball hoop in the driveway and swimming pool in the backyard. It was almost always messy, yet we were made to clean furiously for those visits, keeping up the facade that the shopkeeper in Australia could have the house of the millionaire in Singapore. It was affirmation to my parents in the nineties that the act of migration was worth it.

The lack of maintenance on this house was so extreme that if lights went out, they would stay out for months. The white paper lanterns in the living room were hung so high that for my entire life there, in the 30-odd years my parents had the house, they never changed the paper lantern shades once. These shades became off-white, moth-eaten globes, like the moon would look if it was held against a heavily cobwebbed sky. But even these lanterns outlived my father. They must have spent every penny they had on this place and didn't calculate the expensive cost of handymen in Australia because the house started going downhill from the day it was bought. By 2013, this huge house was literally filled with things. I just thanked God that the ceilings were high, and she could still breathe in the communal areas as a result. There were troublingly strange things to collect, like bolts of quilting fabric and cheap shoes from discount stores. My mother would fill one room with these things until it was bursting, like trying to roll a sleeping bag back into its impossibly tight sheath. If she couldn't sleep in a room anymore, she would pull out her mattress and move into the next room, and then the next room, like a hermit crab changes its shell. Here was her unraveling illustrated in piles of stuff, a topographic map of disconnection from the world. This process continued until that day when she had failed to show up for dinner and was found lying at the bottom of the shower.

The cleaning went on for five months until I got to ground zero, where all the loneliness had begun: my mom and dad's master bedroom, where they had slept side by side for 35 years. Where she had locked herself in during my childhood for consecutive afternoons. Where she had drenched pillows in her tears after Dad's death. That room.

Containers Full of Sadness

I'm small. Just five foot one. I walked to the door, heart pounding in fear of what I'd find in there. The five months preceding had already yielded so much horror. Pushing the master bedroom door open and peering up through the crack between it and the doorframe, I could see the random things piled high above my head height. Magazines, clothes, shoes. A heavy, broken mattress looking like it had been thrown into the air and left to land wherever. It pinned the door closed against me as I pushed, resisting me. It wanted to keep the room's secrets hidden.

I took a deep breath and told myself, 'Simone, no one else can do this but you; this is the last gift you give to your parents.' It truly was. So, I got to work and started cleaning. The most sinister things I found were towers of disposable plastic takeout containers. We may laugh, because we all know an ethnic lady who keeps these takeaway containers. But my mom wasn't domestic. She cooked maybe five times for us in our whole childhood. My dad though was this incredible Chinese cook. He would make vats of Hokkien mee, a fantastic Singaporean noodle dish teeming with seafood, and then make me go with these same disposable takeaway containers to our neighbors. And I'd say in the thick Aussie accent I had then, 'This is really lame, but my dad made noodles.' And push the recycled plastic container, still warm with leftovers, across the threshold of their doorway and into the hands of our Australian neighbors, cocking my head to the side like I was too cool to be doing this. That's how we connected with people – through the shared love of food. Food is love for Asians.

And I realized that my mother was keeping those containers for a time that would never come again: the parties my dad used to cook all those noodles for, wiping beads of sweat from his forehead as he tossed the wok in his polo shirt and slippers. She was waiting for the grandchildren she thought would appear one day. Never had a stack of empty plastic containers felt so heavy with meaning. It was this way with many objects I found in the house.

I kept cleaning until I got to carpet level. There were three bags. One bag was full of every obituary on my father's death that had ever been written in a newspaper, clipping after clipping after clipping. Another plastic bag was full of his X-rays, and the third plastic bag was full of every condolence card she had ever gotten, consoling her on his death.

I sat on the carpet and thought, *From the day Dad died, April 6, 2004, this poor woman, my mother, had stopped throwing anything away.* When we talk about empty nest syndrome, it's deeper than we think. Some mothers, like mine, fill the hollowness with stuff, hoping it embraces them and distracts from the emptiness of missing their children. I recently called my mom about the work I do on human connection and asked her, 'What was it like, Mom, after I left for Dubai and Tamara and I grew up?'

'It was like my world crumbled. I'd go out to the shops and buy things, cheap things, but at least I could talk to people there,' she admitted.

The Bathtub That Broke Me

Cleaning the bathtub was what finally broke me mentally; it pushed me to my knees both literally and metaphorically. This bathtub had long been clogged with dark standing water and shopping receipts floating on top of it. I took another deep breath and sighed, saying to myself again, 'No one else is going to do this but you; this is the last gift you give your parents.' I slapped on the rubber glove and plunged my hand into the water to take the plug out. And that's a moment I'll never forget because every time I do dishes now with rubber gloves on and can feel the water, I'm taken back to this moment.

This is the moment that I lost any remaining connection with myself. Only six months before, I had been a creative, creating radio shows and writing interviews and launching social media campaigns, but I was now a full-time cleaner, and there's absolutely nothing wrong with that. It's good, honest work, but it wasn't what I specialized in or was trained for. In that moment, hearing the sound of the water gurgling out of the tub, I forgot who I was. I had no healthy human connection in my life besides visits to the nursing home to see Mom. My identity dissolved into my gloves in that sludgy black bathtub and didn't emerge again for another half a decade. I had become totally isolated from other people by the act of cleaning the hoard.

The Science Behind Less Touch

One of the first things I felt during this most lonely period in my life was a lack of touch. When you're single and have no friends, as I was in this scenario, there wasn't anyone around to embrace. As we look into a hybrid future long-term, how will our lives be affected by a future with less touch? Where we all work from home and our children will possibly be spending all their social time in metaverses?

Dr. James Coan, Director of the Virginia Affective Neuroscience Laboratory at the University of Virginia, spoke to me about the importance of touch. He told me that touch is powerful because it communicates to our brains that we have more resources beyond ourselves, reminding us of the human tribe we're part of and the safety that comes with being in numbers:

> *The first thing that not having touch is going to do to you is make you more anxious because one of the purposes of touch is to tell your brain that it has less work to do when it comes to being vigilant for potential threats. It's not just any touch, but if it's your partner who's touching you and you have a trusting, high-quality relationship, then your brain is going, 'OK, it's not just my two eyes here that are watching the world. It's also my partner's.'*[33]

We need touch to make us feel safer. So, in a lonely world where individuals are increasingly siloed and deprived of touch, we'll experience less calm. And, as we've seen, higher stress, the antithesis of calm, leads to many life-shortening diseases.

The Costs of Loneliness

What are some of the other costs besides missing human touch? The costs of what I've termed the 'secret loneliness pandemic.' Anxiety and depression are certainly part of it. We are going to see a global mental health crisis over the next few years as the ripples of the effects of social distancing reach outwards. As I mentioned earlier in this book, I lost one of my dearest friends to suicide during the height of the first wave, and similar losses have been seen over and over again during the pandemic.

This could be because loneliness creates a cycle, leading to more isolation. Here's how Dr. Coan explains what's happening in our lonely brains:

What happens when you're lonely is that you become starved. It's like being malnourished. You are constantly running in a kind of deficit with that bioenergetic resource. And so, your brain starts looking for ways to not spend any energy. So, you sleep all day, you avoid anything that seems like it might cause you another stress response, and that avoidance becomes a cycle and you become isolated.

When we're lonely, the stakes become higher and what we do is we paradoxically hold people to higher standards, even though we need people desperately. We require more evidence that they're really going to be there for us. And that keeps us trapped in a cycle of loneliness because we hold people very often to a higher standard than is reasonable.[34]

The second cost of social isolation is social awkwardness. What Dr. Coan describes is really the beginnings of the outbursts and misreading of social cues; this social awkwardness naturally then repels connection. Your social skills, like muscles in your body, atrophy when not being used. A *New York Times* article with the teaser 'We're All Socially Awkward Now' described these symptoms as oversharing on office video calls because you're so thirsty for connection, wanting so badly to be around people.[35] Once around them, however, you want to retreat.

Loneliness Creating More Loneliness

As Dr. Coan and that *New York Times* article describe, loneliness creates a social awkwardness, a yearning to be around others but a retreating, as well as a holding of others to unreasonably high standards. I remember when this started happening within me. I started by finding reasons not to connect with new people. I told myself there was no other 30-year-old with a father in the grave and a mother in a wheelchair, and no one could possibly understand me. I used these falsehoods to hold other people to ridiculously high standards, assuming they could never empathize with me on first meeting. And then, if I went to buy a loaf of bread, I'd tell the lady at the bakery my whole life story.

Oversharing is also a form of social awkwardness and a symptom of loneliness, which we touched on in Chapter 3. Brené Brown states powerfully: 'We have to own our story and share it with someone who has earned the right to hear it.'[36]

Another symptom of my loneliness I mentioned was the misreading of social cues. I'd have rageful outbursts to ethnic aunties visiting my mom's nursing home wielding old-world platitudes about their friends who had strokes and how their Lord, Jesus Christ, saved them. *They didn't have the intel I had*, I thought. I knew what the doctors said. I raged against their opinions and interferences. I had no compassion for their well-intended, but hollow messages.

I started painting at home alone and drinking Moscato at noon. I yearned to be invited out to dinner with people my own age, but the extension of an invite yielded stress. I was immediately scared about whether I'd say something inappropriate. Could I keep a lid on my crazy? I was so out of practice socializing that, once there, I immediately wanted to withdraw and be alone on the rare occasion I was out.

If these symptoms can happen to me, one of the most social people you'll ever meet, they can happen to absolutely anyone, and COVID-19 and its social distancing saw our social skills on a global level atrophy. But like a muscle, we can flex them and get them back. In fact, I think you'll agree it's been amazing watching how quickly humanity has bounced back. For me, and the work that I do, that's just another indication of how innate to us connecting with other humans is.

So, here are some connection challenge points we can put into action to cope with the 'social recession,' as Dr. Coan terms it.[37]

Share more deeply

Talk about deeper things among your existing friends and family. In our current hybrid way of working, where we'll be circulating more amongst our existing connections, we have to connect more authentically to get the health benefits of the connection we need.

Speak your truth

Speaking truthfully doesn't just mean telling your story; it also means being transparent. Speaking transparently can help others in your intimate circle know where you are emotionally and connect with you authentically. But always remember, just because you can say it, should you? Try this week to answer honestly when asked 'How are you?' by an existing connection.

Where you can, make new connections with new people

We get dopamine, the reward hormone, every time we do something pleasurable like eating chocolate, hugging a puppy, or making new connections. They could be your barista; they could be a new neighbor who has moved in next door. Acknowledge these micro-connections, give them that oxytocin-inducing eye contact and help boost their (and your) 'social integration', which, as we saw on page 28, also helps you live longer.[38] Having interactions with a hobby group, speaking to and being seen by your neighbors, or even how many people you talk to during the day all help your mental and physical well-being.

Touch your loved ones more

Oxytocin isn't just the social bonding hormone; it's also the touch hormone. We need it. Remote work threatens to deprive us of our quota long term. So, within your homes, hug your children more, hold your partner's hand, make a concerted effort to do more of it. Make it your mission to embrace your family this week.

Chapter 7

FORGIVE

The Power of Apologizing in Relationships

I grew up in a household that never said 'sorry'. After some of my mom's most blistering menopausal outbursts, or what I now think could have been symptoms of her disease – which as a child were met at first by terror but later, as a teenager, with contempt – there was never a 'sorry'. Arguments with my father where she fought dirty were never met with an apology, only him storming out red-faced to drive his car alone along the West Coast Highway and returning hours later, calm. My father knew something about the power of words or actions you can never take back. Of course he did; his own father had been an alcoholic, and he had grown up with so much of his own trauma. It always seemed to me that when he turned on his heel, still in his work clothes, exhausted after a long day, to exit the house again for relief, he made this conscious decision as a gift to us kids. So we wouldn't have to 'unhear' any more shouting or meanness. I love him for this, but I also now realize he buried that rage, his emasculation, deep inside him for decades and it later emerged with stage IV cancer that began in his kidneys. That's what unresolved rage creates – a disconnection between you and the words you want to say and the feelings you need to get out; your body corrodes and 'dis-ease becomes disease.'

I even remember when my sister and I fought, hurt each other, and clawed at each other as kids. We never did that American TV thing, where our parents made us stand facing each other in the living room to say 'sorry' to each other. I thought hard about it while writing this chapter and realized that any thoughts about apologizing must have been implanted by foreign media. It wasn't just how we fought; it was that we often threw below-the-belt punches – name-calling and put-downs at the things that we knew would hurt the other person deeply. This acidic tongue protected me in high school and when I entered the media industry, but it's also what surfaces when I'm at the lowest integration of myself, when I'm tired and agitated. It's as if, once meanness passes your lips, you never get that innocence back.

How I Finally Learned to Apologize

The woman who taught me to apologize is someone whose name I don't know. I mentioned this story in the introduction. Her hair had slight gray flecks; it flicked out at the side in a long pixie crop. She spoke with a thick South African accent. I was working during my university days at that same sports store I mentioned in Chapter 3. I must have been way too social at this job because I forgot to remove the security tags when I went to scan her clothes at the cash register. During my usual weekly shift, I was behind the counter at the back of the store and saw a woman come in. She looked familiar, swinging her bags with our large logo on them between the racks of clothes. She stormed up to the counter and whacked the bag on the table. I heard the clank of the plastic security tags as she did so. My heart sank. I knew what I'd done – or rather, what I'd forgotten to do. She started to remove the clothes, her angry hands trembling, and muttered, 'You left these tags on my clothes. I don't have time for this. I don't have time for this.'

Having now grown into an adult, I realize that life in Singapore and Dubai is made easier for us because we can hire domestic help, and how this contrasted with the one and a half years I returned to Perth for Mom. I now see fully why she was so stressed; I understand the amount of time that people lose running a household, cleaning, and ferrying kids to school on top of their work without help. I can now fully empathize with this woman's exhaustion. However, as a child who lived in a messy house and had what I perceived as a mother who didn't clean or ferry us anywhere, all I remember was feeling my heart sink to the pit of my stomach as I recognized the garments and knew it was my mistake.

I saw her receipt with my login name on it, the serif font searing my mistake into me, turning me red-faced. I, of course, said I was sorry, but I think this apologizing I did with my non-Asian friends was almost sociopathic. It was said because I knew it was culturally appropriate. Without ever seeing the deep healing value in an apology, I apologized not because I grasped the huge inconvenience this was to her, the time it took away from her parenting, or the stress it caused her. No, I apologized like a chicken so that I wouldn't get in trouble. Her anger also seemed to diffuse my guilt around this; her anger made me more worried than remorseful.

She grabbed the clothes, and just as quickly as she had stormed into the store, she began storming out. But just before she exited, she paused mid-stride, turned back on her heels, and walked up to me. I was hiding now behind a rack of clothes, pretending to neaten them. The lady made a beeline for me behind that rack of clothes. She stopped and looked at me, placed her hand on my shoulder, almost teary-eyed, and said, 'Look, I'm really sorry for getting angry at you. It's just been a really bad day.'

I looked directly into this woman's eyes and saw that rare thing we can never really see in social media videos and pictures. Sincerity. I finally saw it, exactly what a sincere apology looks like, how it felt and resonated through my body. Immediately, all the stress and fear I was feeling dissolved. My hands on that rack stopped trembling.

A sincere apology is one of the greatest tools you can have for healing disconnection in your most treasured relationships. You're not always apologizing because you did something wrong. Of course, if you have, then you should. You're not apologizing for yourself or the space you take up, and we'll discuss this more in a moment. You're apologizing for any hurt that you might have caused to the person. This lady who was my customer didn't do anything wrong, I was at fault, but she was apologizing to me because she might have hurt me. Sometimes our greatest teachers are not our parents or mentors. They are strangers who come into our lives for reasons only the universe has designed.

Apologizing and I have had a more tumultuous and long-term relationship than most of my actual romantic relationships. There were years between when I was full of rage, where I was the woman in the shop. We had swapped places, and I forgot to be the child who learnt this lesson. I fought a war against myself, and everyone around me. I hurt many and didn't say 'sorry' because I was engulfed in a battle being waged in my head. Still, it took moving back to Singapore in 2015 and being embedded in a workplace whose dynamics reminded me of my upbringing, to make the importance of apologizing stand front and center in my life again. I found that 'sorry' was also, like the household I grew up in, not as culturally embedded as in the West.

Allergic to the Word 'Sorry'

Recently, at a Michelin-starred French restaurant in Singapore, I was given a glass straw with the previous user's gunk literally still inside it. Sitting in my Coke. The waitress replaced it, but the word 'sorry' was never uttered. No apology at all. At my former workplace, rife with politics and backstabbing of the level we're used to seeing in Korean dramas, I was the new social threat. This meant I was fair game for bias, snide, anti-foreigner comments mumbled by other presenters, and double-standard rules, like being made to do extra work when others weren't. My boss would shame me on the office group WhatsApp chat for an on-air mistake while I was still live on the air, making sure she could twist the knife in deep while listening to me simultaneously to see if it affected my on-air performance. Everything was so underhanded that it shocked me because I'm dangerously comfortable being transparent and honest, as you can probably tell from this book.

I later learnt that people rarely said what they actually meant in these sorts of work environments – the meaning was between the lines. Apologizing and specifically using the word 'sorry' was taken as an admission of guilt. I was punished for using what my value system told me was an appropriate apology. If I sincerely made a mistake or thought I offended someone, I would apologize. Then an email would be cc'd to almost half of the HR department. I thought many times as the mechanics of the place unveiled itself, *Wow, I should never have emailed sorry for something so small.* Apologies were thought of and treated like you were admitting you were incompetent, and this mistake held crushing disciplinary consequences, mostly consisting of public shaming. By the time two years had passed, I remember thinking, *You must get out of here before you are changed forever by this place.*

So, it's no wonder that no one conceded an apology when a mistake was made. The body language of guilt and sometimes remorse was there, but the words were never uttered, much like my mother after her outbursts. Sometimes food was given in its place. Buying us a cake because the word 'sorry' was like an allergy. After posting about this on social media, so many commented, 'This is amazing. I'm so glad to have heard this, and it really is an eye-opener and shifts certain ideologies of how sorry/apologizing has always been used this entire time. Thank you.' Or, 'I've learnt something so important from this. Sorry isn't always an admission of incompetence. It's also a recognition of the other person's feelings and dignity. Thanks, Simone.' Or, 'As Asians battle, we never say sorry.'

Remorse

When I was a child at school, a picture book was given to us at age seven called *The Meanies*. In the book, a group of rather terrifying looking trolls doled out mean behavior to people in their community. After closing the book, my third-grade teacher looked up at us and said, 'What the Meanies didn't have was remorse. Remorse is that feeling after you've done something, and you feel bad because you know you shouldn't have done it.'

I knew the exact feeling she was speaking about. This is how I first came to identify remorse, and later guilt, and how it feels in my body. It'll feel different for you. When you feel remorse or guilt, you may feel it in your gut like I do, or it could be in your lower back or even in your brain base. What's important is that you know it when you feel it and take action on it, if needed.

Apologizing Connects Us

When we say 'sorry,' we build deeper connections with family and friends because it's risky. That risk and exposure make it an act of vulnerability. An apology is a prerequisite for forgiveness, but we aren't guaranteed forgiveness, or that our apology is accepted simply by saying 'sorry.' The lack of pride it takes to apologize demonstrates that we value the connection over our own ego. As we discussed in that earlier chapter, connection deepens from vulnerability. An apology is like scar tissue; it sits over a wound and allows it to close over and heal. It can be seen on our skin like a reminder – like the word 'sorry' hangs in the air between you and that person you love. We remember and are grateful to the people who apologized for hurting us. It connects us.

'Sorry' is one of the most powerful things you can say to the people you love to diffuse hurt and bring harmony back. In a *Harvard Mental Health Letter* article titled, 'Learning How to Say, "I'm Sorry"', apologies are described as 'a prerequisite for forgiveness,' and forgiveness is key to healing and maintaining healthy human connections.[39] I think any of us who want to live peaceful lives have forgiven many people for hurting us without an apology being verbalized. I think that's helpful too, but when there are active connections in our orbits that we want to nurture and maintain, having a good, sincere 'sorry reflex' can serve us well. It is simply needed to maintain connections, like watering a plant when the soil gets too dry.

If we know all this, why is apologizing so difficult for us? Apologizing is nothing short of terrifying. TERRIFYING. It's one of the actions in our lives that requires a huge amount of vulnerability because acceptance of your apology is never guaranteed. The reason apologies are so healing is also because of this same emotional risk. When someone makes themselves sincerely vulnerable to us, it's a gift. I describe it as ripping your heart out and placing it on a silver platter on the floor between you and another person, hoping they don't step on it. This is why truly apologizing is so scary. We lose the psychological safety we're wired to crave as human beings, but it's so worth doing if you treasure your human connections.

Now that you know how it works and why it makes you feel the way you do, I hope it diffuses some of the sting of doing it. Here are my connection challenges:

Apologize to others with sincerity

A sincere apology isn't sarcastic. Dr. Aaron Lazare, an expert on apologies, says, 'Good apologies can foster healing, but a bad apology only makes a bad situation worse.'[40]

An apology prefaced by 'I'm sorry you feel that way' doesn't validate your involvement in the hurt caused, but rather gaslights the other person into feeling they only perceived the hurt. It's a terrible way to add fuel to the fire.[41]

Discern who the people are in your tribe who may need an apology from you

Here's a quick exercise to reveal people you may need to apologize to. Scroll through the most frequently used messaging app on your phone. Look at each person's name and think of them. If you arrive at a person's name where you stop and feel some energy that's not so positive, it may be a sign you need to offer an apology. I want you to really go deep. Close your eyes and think of how you feel each time you've interacted with this person. Have you maybe had a disagreement, an angry email, a bad breakup, or a harsh word with them in the past? Now it's time to take ownership over the unsaid apology, that thing that hangs in the air like an open wound. I've reached out and done this a few times in my life to people who deserved an apology; it's scary, but so worth it. Do know that not everyone will respond or accept it, but if you're still in contact with them, the probability is quite high that they will.

Recognize when you don't need to say 'sorry'

Boundaries for apologizing are just as important as apologizing. Just like we don't have to connect with everyone all the time to be good human connectors, we also don't have to apologize for every single thing we do, or for the act of being ourselves. In 2015, in the wake of therapy, as the process wore me down and recalibrated me, I hadn't secured my boundaries yet. Everything was in flux. As a result of this, I let many people into my life I wouldn't now, and tolerated unbelievably bitchy behavior from people I wouldn't now. I was apologetic for everything, including just being me. I look back at some of the nasty people during that time, and I know with assuredness that I don't owe them an apology and that we're better off not being in one another's orbits. This includes family, which is really difficult for me to say as an Asian woman. I was conditioned to tolerate everything from bitchiness, verbal abuse, and harsh gossip from aunties, cousins, and more. After therapy, the breaking down and building myself back up, I now have really clear boundaries. Think about your own relationship boundaries. Do you find yourself apologizing just for being you?

More reparations if needed

Look at the ways the hurt was caused. If the hurt caused may have been meant to embarrass or cause shame, then apologize to restore dignity and heal any hurt. But if there has been some sort of loss or damage to property, there need to be additional reparations. If you scraped another parent's car at the schoolyard, then apologizing for it and offering to pay for the damage is more sincere.

The best way to begin approaching an apology is by looking at the offense. Is the apology worded in a way that reflects the offense? For example, infidelity in a partnership would see the wording of the apology with a tone that marks the gravity of the offense. You wouldn't use the same language to apologize for leaving the toilet seat up as you would for cheating on your spouse. Eye contact, body language, and emotion (we'll talk about that more in a coming chapter) all communicate remorse just as powerfully as words. Following the apology, there should be steps to remedy the behavior. Here's an example in the case of a cheating spouse: 'I know I can't take back what I've done. It was terrible. I'm so sorry. I'm committed now to being here at home, focusing on our time together, and seeing a couples' therapist with you.'

By apologizing in the right way and focusing on providing healing for the person we've hurt, we can more comprehensively maintain the health of our most valued relationships.

Loving-kindness meditation

This ancient form of meditation has been a wonderful tool for me. It may help you to create some peace for yourself over pain between you and another when you can't access them. Maybe they have passed on, or the pain is just too deep right now. It can prepare you for the bravery needed to reach out and apologize, or even calm the knowledge that you may not receive an apology yourself.

Although it's been in existence for thousands of years in many Eastern religions, we're lucky today to be able to access loving-kindness meditation for free by a simple search online. What is so powerful about this practice is that the meditation begins by directing your love to yourself, then to someone you have neutral feelings about, then to someone where there may be some resentment, and finally to all mankind. It is in reflecting on this shift from self to others in relationships that we can get clarity on where we're at with someone. The meditation also helps to break down the wall between us and other people, reminding us that, actually, we're all one.

In her book *Love 2.0*, Barbara L. Fredrickson describes how her Positive Emotions and Psychophysiology Laboratory tested participants who practiced loving-kindness meditation and she presented these findings to His Holiness the 14th Dalai Lama.[42] The results? Those participants who had devoted scarcely an hour each week to the practice had their vagus nerve (the nerve that regulates heart rate, breathing, and blood pressure, among other functions) respond more quickly to their breathing – evidence that the practice literally improves your physical health.

Chapter 8

RAPPORT

Building
Connection
by Meeting
People
Where
They Are

The newsagent's shop where my father worked seven days a week for almost 20 years secured us our residency in Australia and provided us with school fees, holidays to Singapore, and that very exchange trip to Switzerland that changed my entire worldview. In the nineties, a time when people still needed stationery, I loved watching my father serve his customers. During school holidays, when the rest of my peers were out at the beach or going to the cinema, I would be sent to shadow my dad in the shop. My mother thought if I learnt to count back change manually, I'd become better at math in school. What she didn't count on was the fact my dad was deeply compassionate.

The minute he heard the beads of gravel crunch under the tires of my mother's car as she reversed out of the shopping center parking lot, my dad would allow me to step back from the counter, stop working, and read all the outdated magazines he kept. I would sit cross-legged on the carpet behind his counter surrounded by piles of *Smash Hits* and *Archie* comics, devouring the content. Ironically, as we now know, this wouldn't be the last time I'd be surrounded by piles of magazines taller than my head height. On these blissful magazine-sorting afternoons, though, as a nine-year-old, I'd get bored of reading after a few hours, and then I'd look up and observe my dad serving his customers. His newsagent's shop, also prophetically, was opposite a nursing home. I'd watch older adults on scooters zip over to buy scratch cards. These people – many of them migrants or even orphans brought to Western Australia to work when they were young – had the most incredible stories. I knew these stories because my dad (and Mom too, on the occasions she helped Dad in the shop) would listen to the elderly when the shop was slow, providing social interaction for them and a place to spend a couple of dollars. It was my father's incredible knack for building rapport almost instantly that primed his customers, making them feel safe to engage in self-disclosure. After my father's death, we found he had given many of these people unlimited tabs that were never paid when they passed away. He truly loved people, and that love was underpinned by empathy and compassion. I strive to be more like him every day.

I remember watching how my father, standing at the counter, would open an interaction every time a new customer came in. Every time I think of him, I just think of the word 'humble.' In fact, the only time he wasn't – the only time he exhibited something else in his character – was in the wake of his cancer diagnosis. Then, he became enraged, not because that was his personality, but because he was pissed off at the universe for not allowing him to stay longer.

When I say my dad was characterized by the word 'humble,' it's because he wore his humble beginnings in the way he carried himself – shoulders turned slightly down and inwards. Even though Australia was a fresh start, where new migrants could wipe the slate of their backgrounds clean, and no one would know how you were raised, Dad still had this body language that appeared reluctant to take up space. Or maybe it was because my mother seemed to be the opposite, bordering on haughty to those who didn't know her brilliance. Maybe he was just trying to balance them out as a couple. Slight in build and short, my father always dressed in formal slacks – despite the warm Australian weather – with a belt with the letter 'H' embossed on the buckle. This belt is the one possession of his I've taken all around the world with me to remember him by. It was certainly no Hermés; it simply stood for 'Heng.'

I'd listen intently to what my father would say to his customers, who would vary profoundly in age and background. He would honor them by always talking about the things they wanted to talk about. If a new Malaysian migrant customer came in, my father would lean deep into his hips, giving off a casual air, and thicken his Asian accent, throw words of Chinese dialect in. The switch almost said, 'I know I've been in Australia over a decade; I know I've raised my family here, but I'm still like you, my Asian brother.' Then the two men would all-out debate which country had the best laksa, Singapore or Malaysia. Then, like a switch, as decisively as traffic lights turn from red to green, if his German migrant customer came in, a man who had been in Australia for two decades, my father would neutralize his accent, mirror the man's upright posture, and talk about the Eurovision Song Contest. God, we loved Eurovision! (For the unacquainted, the Eurovision Song Contest is an American Idol-style competition that spans the European countries, with each country competing with a song. Countries vote on each other's songs, and it can become very political. It's known for some truly quirky and over-the-top submissions.)

My father neutralizing his accent wasn't an attempt to put on airs or to negate his Asian-ness. Rather it was a simple attempt to be understood more quickly through clarity of communication and this expedited connection. In so doing, he made it far less work for his customers to connect with him. When a British customer came in, my father would keep his accent neutral and talk at length about the English Premier League and break down the latest match play by play. I often wondered why he would allow me to stay up later in the Aussie winter and crack chestnuts in bed watching these matches. My father was a golf fan himself; it's what he played, so it was strange to me to make this effort to watch football as well. He was doing it to make sure he always had content to draw from to connect with his customers because, as an immigrant trying to eke out a living, the stakes for human connection were still about survival, the same way they were for us as early humans living in tribes. He knew those customers kept the warm chestnuts in my hands, the rice bowl in my stomach, and the overpriced private-school uniform on my back.

Over the years, regular customers, like his British one, came to trust my father deeply because of his consistent choice to be of service in his communication. He would, in a sense, inconvenience himself, his need to talk about whatever he wanted to talk about, in the language or accent of his preference, to make others feel served. To make others feel welcomed and have their stories validated. I learnt quickly that true connection happens when others feel seen and heard. These small tweaks in communication allowed my dad's customers to perceive him as one of them, a member of their tribe. Once rapport was established, he built trust by consistently showing up in this way over the course of two decades. The rapport my father built created a deep trust, which allowed long-term connection to happen.

I also realized that watching my dad serve customers, pivoting his communication, learning the interests of others, and neutralizing his accent subconsciously became the backbone of my broadcasting career. In my 15 years in radio, I worked on the mic for stations in Dubai, Australia, and Singapore. To this day, I don't know any other radio DJ in the world who has done that, because radio is a notoriously local medium. It prides itself on its insularity. So I had, effectively, been paid to persuade people in three hugely diverse markets that I could speak to their heartbeat. I learnt this from Robert Heng.

Almost exactly a decade after those school holidays sitting in the shop and watching him, beads of gravel once again crunched under the tires of a car in that shopping center parking lot. This time the car was the hearse carrying my father's body on the morning of his funeral. Because Dad worked so much, Mom had decided to have us drive my father's daily routine from home to work, before finally ending up at the church for the service. I remember it being a cold morning, pressing my pimply 19-year-old cheek against the cool glass of that car window, and looking out to see a sea of people, some of them bank employees from the bank where my dad put his float in for the day, dressed in their fresh workday outfits; Leslie, the pharmacist, wearing her crisp, white lab coat, Harry, my dad's best friend, the Greek man who owned the fish-and-chip shop, the pallbearer for my dad's casket. And there, up the back, stood his German customer, his Malaysian customer, his British customer. They showed up for their humble local shopkeeper at the end of his life. This is how I know this approach to connection works.

Building Rapport

In his book *The Art of Reading Minds*, author Henrik Fexeus says the basic rule of rapport is to 'adapt to how the other person communicates' versus imposing what you want to talk about and how you want to talk about it.[43] Good rapport is magic because it says to people 'we're more alike than you think.' It allows people to feel closer to us and this establishes trust more quickly.

Here's another analogy for rapport building that may make you see this not as an act of trickery or mimicry, but one of humble service. One of the human connection superheroes I interviewed for my TEDx Talk on the power of human connection was a teacher at the leading school for children with autism in Singapore. She mentioned to me that UDL, the universal design for learning, helped her connect with her students, regardless of where on the spectrum they were. Instead of a test, students could submit an artistic map of what they'd learnt, or deliver a talk. UDL is an approach in teaching that advocates for equal opportunity for all students by giving students multiple means of expression of what they have learnt and multiple means of accessing material so they can choose what works best for them. UDL has proven to be a more inclusive way of teaching and connecting with students, allowing students to be met where they are. It's a brilliant analogy for the kind of rapport-building communication my father specialized in – meeting people not halfway, but 80 percent of the way. This is something we can all emulate in a world thirsty for connection.

Here are some connection challenges for building rapport:

Use your body to connect

Like my father did over the counter, adopting the same body posture as his customers, use your body to mirror the stance of the person you're trying to connect with. This sends a reassuring message to their brain that 'this person is like me.'

My dad did a great deal of communicating with his body, despite being cordoned off by his shop counter. Just as we experience during virtual conferences today, he only had his upper body to communicate with. Mirroring is also valuable for digital communication: frame the bottom of your laptop screen when on a virtual conference to the triangle of hard muscle where your rib cage meets: this is your diaphragm. By having your hands in the shot, you build trust with your audience. As humans, we're suspicious of concealed hands (hands behind the back when speaking to a live audience or below a desk when doing virtual presentations). This goes back to our hunter-gatherer days, where our brains became wired to check immediately that a stranger wasn't holding a weapon in their hands that could hurt us. Vanessa Van Edwards states in her TEDx Talk *You Are Contagious* that it's exactly because of this survival mechanism that, to this day, the first thing we do when we meet a new person is glance at their hands.[44] So to build trust and connection, frame your virtual screen wider to include your arms and your upper torso.

Harness the power of your voice

If the person is a quiet speaker, match their volume level. If they speak a language you speak as well, switch to theirs. If they speak English as a second language and struggle to understand, slow your own speech down. Make it easier for the other person on any level to connect with you more quickly, meeting them more than halfway.

Inconvenience yourself

Try putting aside your needs to discuss what you want to talk about in initial meetings with a new connection. Just listen, soak up who the person is first, and then connect with them on the topics they prefer, where you have some common ground. Eventually, when trust and rapport are established, they should come and ask you more about yourself, too.

Be on the lookout for things to connect on

I often get asked how to connect with a new person in this way if they don't disclose anything about themselves. Great human connectors know that connection leaves clues, so scan for commonalities constantly. I'd often see my dad glance at a customer's attire and see them wearing a cap emblazoned with their favorite sports team's logo. He would then rattle off any trivia he knew about this team or the sport they played to begin the conversation. Prime yourself to look for connection points when you're at your next social gathering or virtual meeting. What clues can you see that you could connect on?

Chapter 9

UNMASKED

The Power of Facial Expressions in Connection

It's 2013 and I stand at a radio panel. 'Safe and Sound' by Capital Cities is playing, blasting out of the radio speakers. My eyes are watching the radio log on a computer screen, which in itself is like reading a real-time music chart with an electronic list of songs and digital buttons. If you toggle just one of those elements incorrectly, it will make a song end, skip, and even mix two highly recognizable songs together on an unlucky day. I say 'highly recognizable' because the station I'm working at in Dubai is a huge brand, and it plays Top 40 hits. The tunes play on repeat until they get inside you, and you find yourself pumping gas nodding your head.

This particular song, still relatively new, is by two Armenian brothers in LA. I'm noting this down on paper, prepping in my head to back sell the song after it stops in 60 seconds. 'Back selling,' I've been taught, is to describe something interesting about the song in retrospect. But then my thoughts are hijacked like a home invader has run into my head and scooped up the entire contents of my skull in his hands and run back out my ear. All I hear is a kind of tinny white noise. I'm out of my own body

139

because the surging medieval horns of the song and otherwise upbeat lyrics about safety amid calamity can't make peace with what I'm feeling inside.

This, I now know, is what's called a trigger. Thirty seconds to go before the song ends, I'm sobbing, because the last thing I feel is 'safe' or 'sound'. I've been back in Dubai for a week after returning from three weeks in Australia following my mom's stroke. This very afternoon, I'm going to go in to resign from my dream job of half a decade. This brand I gave my life to. The image of my mother, gray-skinned and terrified, lying at the bottom of the shower, curled inward onto herself like a snail, is all I see. She's all alone. The guilt and shame are unbearable. That stroke, I didn't know then, would lead her to sit in her waste for the rest of her life. Ten seconds. I blow my nose, stand up straight at the panel, and smile my largest, happiest smile because I know people will hear it in my voice. That's what I've been taught. I still believe the smile is to the voice what eye contact is to the face. It primes for connection.

I disconnect my needs, my sorrow, and the fight-or-flight response for just a moment. I tell myself, 'It's connection time with others now.' Give the audience what they want. That's what I've been conditioned to do my whole adult life. Five, four, three, two, one. The song stops.

'It's 104.4 Virgin Radio Dubai. This is Simone Heng on the Lowdown. Two Armenian brothers out of LA there with their surging lyrics, new to the playlist it's "Capital Cities"...'

My smile widens so I make it through. I'm rushing the talk break; I know it. I tell my mouth to slow down. I remember this telling because that's what fight-or-flight mode does. It makes conscious and deliberate thought feel like labor. I smile harder until I can feel the stretching of skin in the corner of my mouth. I feel tears formed 20 seconds ago drying on my cheeks. Then I continue. That is my job; that's what I've been programmed to do. 'Coming up next, music from Rihanna, David Guetta, and Jay Sean. You're listening to Virgin,' I say.

Emotion From the Outside in

The talk break is over. My chest depresses from being full of air and energy. The skin in the corners of my mouth stretched upward has come back to the place nature intended, curled downwards like deflated birthday balloon rubber. My smile starts to fade again. I'm exhausted. The ads are playing, and while they do, I check in with myself, connect with myself. How do I feel? That's where I can see and feel the difference. I feel marginally better. The act of being forced to change my body language and my facial expressions has actually made me feel happier. Tired, but happier. I shelve this realization in my library of overwhelming thoughts during a crisis.

Half a decade later, I'll learn at a Tony Robbins conference amid euphoric strangers that that's how it works. That we can change our energy, mental state, and mood simply by altering our physicality. Tony gets the entire 20,000-strong crowd to hunch over and mimic the posture of what we think a depressed person may stand like. Then we mimic how we think a confident person would stand. Then he explains to us the science behind Amy Cuddy's power poses, and I realize just how right he is about this.[45] I've been doing my power poses and teaching my clients how to change their state ever since.[46]

The Art of Saving Face

Your facial expressions are the physical manifestation of your emotions. The willingness to express and have mastery over your facial expressions is incredibly powerful, not just for changing your state, as I've described in my on-air story earlier, but also for connecting with others. On the one hand, changing your face, as I did on air, to induce 'happy hormones' into your body can be effective. In that case, it got me through my shift at work that day in that sad moment. But are there, on the other hand, negative implications to our ability to connect with others if we constantly repress our emotions and conceal our facial expressions? This is what we'll explore next.

We all learnt the importance of harnessing the power of facial expressions in a COVID-19, mask-wearing world. However, where I live, in Asia and as an Asian woman, we were wearing masks long before a pandemic. For thousands of years, East Asian people, and particularly East Asian women, have been told to be quiet, mitigate our negative and private feelings (soften our expressiveness), and 'not give too much away.' This results in an almost freezing of the facial expressions, like a culturally infused Botox jab. If we don't express, we don't risk losing our dignity or our family's. What do we give people in its place? We save face. We are taught this from the time we're young because 'losing face' is an almost unbearable insult for many ethnically Chinese people.

As an Asian girl growing up, it wouldn't be unheard of to have my mother or aunties say, 'Eh, don't give so much away,' and 'Be less animated; don't be so crazy.' For me, being expressive was soon associated with being less demure and, therefore, undesirable. The act of not emoting for self-preservation meant that I learnt to equate expressiveness with weakness and to resent the innate expressiveness that has turned out to be the gift of my entire career.

I'd be shushed at home, but empowered to express my emotions at my Australian school. In fact, to get the grades that my parents wanted in this Australian school, I needed to learn to show emotion in class. This created an almost schizophrenic-like code-switching that many Asian children growing up in Western cultures can relate to. At home, we were given approval based on obedience, not expressing an opinion with our mouths or faces. We were commended for not giving too much away about how we felt or what we thought to people outside of our family unit, yet to be understood in the Western context we lived in, we had to learn to express ourselves fully.

A Lack of Expressiveness Can Affect Connection

When we don't emote fully, we run the risk of losing out on a lot of deep, authentic connections for a few reasons. First, people perceive us as less transparent and don't feel safe with us. We also give so little emotional information away that it's hard for people to read us. Through the godfather of mapping facial expressions, Dr. Paul Ekman, we know that the interpretation of all but seven facial expressions differs greatly across cultures.[47] He describes these as universal facial expressions: anger, contempt, disgust, fear, joy, sadness, and surprise. A more recent study in the Trobriand Islands by Boston College Professor of Psychology James A. Russell and colleagues may have called into question the interpretation of the expression of fear as universal; however, Ekman's work on the other expressions is still valuable here.[48]

When we express emotions fully, it allows other people to connect with us more quickly because they have a temperature gauge for what we're thinking. In my last workplace in Singapore before becoming a full-time speaker, I was constantly confused. Any negative emotions were mitigated, a complete swallowing of facial expressions. So, when I first started working there, I could never read if someone was mad at me or if I'd overstepped. I'd only find harsh, reprimanding emails later, but a sweet, neutral expression sold to me in person. There is a part of Asian upbringing, the Chinese part of me knows, that values the concealment of information, and this has many benefits, such as negotiating business contracts.

However, this doesn't serve us as well when connecting in the global context. We are doing business daily with people around the world who are looking at our faces on video conferences and trying to read us.

We have all, regardless of ethnicity, experienced how challenging it's been reading the faces of our fellow humans when we're wearing COVID-19 masks. A total mess of meaning and communication not landing right. One person I know described reading faces with masks on like 'reading a heavily redacted text. Feeling like something important gets missed.' Studies back up her feelings, indicating that masks inhibit the capability to perceive a lot of social information. Furthermore, they make emotions more difficult to interpret and block facial mimicry and behavioral synchrony, lowering social bonds, empathy, and playful interactions.[49]

The more countries I've lived in and the more international our world becomes, the more I've realized that masking our feelings is a direct route to not connecting authentically. If you conceal your emotions and thoughts constantly, people connect with an avatar of you instead of the real you. It also means the vulnerability that comes from the expression of emotions on your face is absent, and vulnerability is how we truly connect. When we show emotion, it builds trust because we demonstrate a transparency that tells other people it's safe to connect.

In summary, facial expressions are powerful tools for connection to change our state and connect with others. Here are some connection challenges to start really activating your facial expressions as a tool for human connection:

Use your facial expressions to improve your mood and feeling

Manipulating your facial expressions as a momentary mood booster isn't a wholly bad thing. In the first story I shared about having to smile on air, even though I felt terrible inside, I wasn't meeting anyone. I just needed a perk-up. If you're having an off-day, do some smiling before you go into work or need to perform in a high-stakes meeting. Smiling when you don't feel happy can trick your brain into believing you feel better than you do. Studies have shown that a smile stimulates the production of dopamine, the feel-good hormone, and serotonin, which is a stress reducer. So, there's science backing why we should smile behind our masks during a time of huge anxiety like the COVID-19 pandemic and its aftermath.[50]

Find out how expressive you actually are

Here's a quick self-connection exercise. Take some selfies of the seven universal expressions: anger, contempt, disgust, fear, joy, sadness, and surprise. Then do a Google search and look at the images of the expressions under each of them. Do your selfies match these? How did expressing these feelings feel for you? Is this something you express naturally, or do you find expressing these emotions foreign, like you haven't exercised them since you were a child? Think about when the last time was that you expressed one of these emotions. Was there a feeling of being totally out of control, or was expressing them a relief? Repressing and not expressing negative emotions to our most intimate connections can mean that those we love don't know how we feel and can't fully support us if we need them.

Practice expressing with your eyes

Eye contact is imperative when building trust. With the mask-wearing we've been made to do for the pandemic, learning to be comfortable giving eye contact is vital. Human beings are naturally suspicious of people who avoid eye contact. Eye contact also produces the social-bonding hormone oxytocin. Make a concerted effort to make eye contact within your household first by looking up from those devices and releasing dopamine, the feel-good hormone.[51] When smiling, make an effort to smile with your eyes, with what is called the 'Duchenne smile' – a smile that crinkles the corners of your eyes and is perceived as sincere by others.

Chapter 10

NOMAD

Learning to Connect from Serial Expatriates

In high school, because of the limiting belief I held that I was 'unlovable,' I'd play a game. As a 13-year-old, I'd see how many people from any grade I could say hello to when we crossed paths in the hallways. Soon I'd see people almost nervous as I approached; they knew I'd be acknowledging them. Their faces would flush as they tried to avoid eye contact, not dissimilar from the subtle social awkwardness and averted gazes we've seen on video conferences during the pandemic. This is a great analogy for how connection can feel since the advent of social media. It's surface-level, it's broad and shallow, and it's often awkward. It's what Arianna Huffington describes as a 'junk food version of connection' that fails to give us the real emotional sustenance that keeps us healthy and happy.[52]

Many Superficial Connections

So what kinds of connection do we actually need? In her TED Talk on connection, Susan Pinker shares Julianne Holt-Lunstad's research and describes the kinds of close relationships we need as 'the people that you can call on for a loan if you need money suddenly, who will call the doctor if you're not feeling well, or who will take you to the hospital, or who will sit with you if you're having an existential crisis.'[53] These are the friendships we should be nurturing as deep connections. When we have a quantity of low-depth human connections and none of the intimate and relational connection, we're at risk of becoming lonely. A life consisting of shallow connection alone simply makes us crave something deeper. A large network is great, provided you also have a bedrock of healthy, quality, intimate connections to support you.

In my mid-20s, when I moved to Dubai, I attended event after event in that city in an attempt to quench my thirst for belonging, and justifying it as great 'networking' for my career. I didn't realize that none of this 'being surrounded by people' would heal my yearning to belong. From the statistics shared in earlier chapters, I believe that a large proportion of the world is also currently searching for more intimate connection. People with whom we can truly be vulnerable.

Christina Sang is a 35-year-old serial expatriate who has lived in the Philippines, France, the United Arab Emirates, Portugal, the USA, the UK, and Switzerland. She was most recently stuck in her current home in Bali for over a year during the pandemic. When living in Dubai, Christina worked in corporate communications for some of the most illustrious hotels. She was also a PR consultant to over a hundred luxury brands in art and culture and select diplomatic events, including taking care of royalty and Hollywood A-listers.

I remember watching Christina when I was a young radio DJ – she was tirelessly and seamlessly connecting with people of all demographics, over and over. Initiating connection is her gift. I have a theory as to why people like Christina and me, who grow up between worlds and multiple cultures, become so zealous about connection. Christina grew up in Manila, but is of Korean ethnicity. She moved to the USA for high school alone and at a young age. She then went to hospitality school in Switzerland, met a boyfriend there, and moved to Portugal with him. She has since lived in Dubai and Bali. People like Christina and me enter the world essentially without our 'tribe,' so our bodies hit us with an urgency that tells us from a very young age: you're alone; you're not safe; go and make your tribe – and we do. This gives us a sense of belonging and social connectedness, and as we grow older and live in multiple countries, these instincts remain. We simply hone our human connection skills more often than most.

I asked Christina about her experience in Dubai creating so many events, where surface-level connections take center stage, and how they made her feel:

I felt like the majority of the people – as I moved my career from hospitality into consultancy and then being in PR, representing luxury brands and royalty – always wanted something from me. So, 90 percent of the time, I'd speak to people on a day-to-day basis that wanted to use me or needed something from me. So, it becomes a vicious cycle, and the promiscuity of those connections is just too much. It's like you have an energy tank for connection, and all that energy is going into meaningless fluff.

Christina's feelings here of 'everybody wanting something from me' was certainly how I felt at times with my work on the radio. Businesses both big and small sidling up to me hoping I'd mention their brands on air, which I absolutely couldn't do for free, anyway; I'd have been fired. There's good science behind why we're wary of such connections. Psychologist and thought leader in the study of loneliness, the late Professor John Cacioppo, says,

If you look at early humans and other hominids, they were not uniformly positive toward each other. We exploit each other, we punish each other, we threaten each other, we coerce. And so it isn't that I want to connect with anyone, I need to worry about friend or foe... If I mistakenly detect someone as a friend when they're a foe, that can cost me my life. Over evolution, we've been shaped to have this bias.... You're motivated to connect. But promiscuous connection with others can lead to death. A neural mechanism kicks in to make you a little skeptical or dubious about connecting.[54]

A Lonely Brain Makes You Lonelier

During those 'networking' years, my social orbits became swollen. I was surrounded by people, giving me the impression I was less alone, but it never really satiated me. After a big breakup, I soon became steeped in intimate loneliness. I craved a partner badly. Some days the love others were finding was hard for me to celebrate, bringing my own unlovability into stark relief. A self-loathing set in. *How could I have dealt with so much suffering in my family life and this one thing I needed, the universe wouldn't give me?* It wasn't a rational thought, but the lonely brain often isn't. It becomes suspicious of everyone, tests friends, and is on high alert for people's betrayal. It becomes a loop. The lonelier you feel, the harder you make it for connection to come into your life.

This is backed by Cacioppo's findings, too.[55] The lonely brain becomes hypervigilant to social threats, many times more than the non-lonely brain. I became sensitive. If a friend canceled, I'd take it as abandonment. If someone was late to meet, it was a deep sign of disrespect, even if they were really good people who had totally understandable reasons for doing so. I'd even be annoyed at every new person who would reach out to connect. If I did meet up with them, I'd soon find fault with them and use it as a reason not to connect with them again. I'm sure many of us go through this but never make the connection that the source could be loneliness. Why would we, if we're surrounded by people wanting to connect with us? The lonely brain is trying to keep you safe but, in the process, makes you more lonely. If you're experiencing this, I write this because I want you to know this is backed by science. You are not alone.

Quantifying Connection

How many connections should we aim to have? In a world where social media followers abound to thousands, according to Robin Dunbar we can only maintain 150 meaningful contacts. Dunbar states:

> *The way in which our social world is constructed is part and parcel of our biological inheritance.... We're members of the primate family – and within the primates there is a general relationship between the size of the brain and the size of the social group. We (human beings) fit a pattern. There are social circles beyond it and layers within – but there is a natural grouping of 150.*[56]

What this tells us is that we can't reasonably maintain more than 150 relationships. 'Dunbar's Number' is valuable because it allows us to assess not only the number of people in our orbits of connection but also to assess what constitutes a 'meaningful contact' in our lives. If you're in that space I was in back in my mid-20s in Dubai, this study can really help you audit your human connections. Are you surrounded by a superfluous network of acquaintances that works not to make you feel a deeper sense of belonging but rather, makes you feel more alone?

Having lived in cities like Perth and St. Gallen, Switzerland, versus Singapore and Dubai, the lack of transience in the former breeds a different sort of connection, which is interesting to understand and can also set fertile ground for deep loneliness for totally different reasons. Loneliness, as we know, is indifferent to location. You can be anywhere and still be lonely. This is something I felt when I repatriated to Australia to care for my mother after a decade of being away.

Resistance to Broadening Established Social Groups

Non-expatriate settings see more people retaining their friendships from as early as primary school. People in these environments seemingly have all the connections they need; there's a permanence in the orbits of their connection. They've gone deep, not wide, like those of us in those transient expat cities.

There is a lot of value in deep connection, but what it also means for those who have had their same tribe for decades, set almost in concrete, is they aren't so keen to start inviting new people to their dinner parties. It's logical; it's how we're wired in our early human brains to keep ourselves safe from the unknown. Upon my repatriation, I became a social threat, rarely invited in or asked to join already established social groups of people my own age. This was so different from how quickly new social connections are tried on for size in expat cities; it literally sent me into a reverse culture shock. The experience for me as a single female was the most socially isolating of my life.

I'm not alone in experiencing this. Heather Hansen, a global communications expert who is from the USA, but has lived as an expat primarily in Singapore and Denmark and did so, unlike me, with both her spouse and children, described the difference between Singapore and moving back to her husband's home in Denmark:

> *It's different because in Denmark there isn't the same expat culture. You are pushed into the local culture much faster than in Singapore. There isn't that divide between 'expat' and 'local' that can be seen in Singapore, as well. And of course, since I was married to a Dane and I speak the language, you would think that I would connect quite easily, but I didn't feel that. I have maybe two good friends of my own that are not through my husband there.*

> *I actually found it very difficult because, in Denmark, people grow up and make their friends at a very young age. And they're still friends with those people as adults. I love my husband's group of friends, and they have fully accepted me, but still it's usually those kinds of group things. It's not that I would call one of them with my problems to have a girl chat. We are very much like a group of friends who do things together, not those personal one-on-one connections.*

Denmark is pretty closed. I was included in my husband's circle because I was married to the culture. I wouldn't have ever been invited into that group any other way. Primarily, because you have your close friends, and you don't really have a need for new friends outside of those circles. I get it, but it does make it very, very difficult to break into a culture.

By now, we know that human beings evolved to value safety in numbers and that people outside the tribe posed a social threat, so it makes sense that we find it hard to let new people in when we feel our social needs are already safely being met. But in the world we now live in, where loneliness is the secret pandemic leading to a mental health crisis, I argue we may have to push past these innate instincts in two distinct ways. First, I hope that those reading this book who feel they have their social connections in place think of ways to challenge themselves to let someone new in. How can you place your own comfort and busyness aside and give your time, even in small ways, to those who feel alone? The rewards of doing so are incredible. A new friend bringing new insights and conversations can be priceless. Second, for those of us who are expats, we can learn to harness some of the depth and stability from these non-expat environments.

Learning to Mimic the Expat Mindset

The other side of expatriate cities, like Singapore, Dubai, and Hong Kong, is that people are separated from their families. To combat the transience of friends leaving constantly, people are much more open to allowing new connections into their fold. This differs from when one permanently migrates to a new place; expats know they won't be there forever. The perception of being a visitor also leads to a feeling of urgency about their time in a particular place, which I didn't experience in non-transient environments. The lack of psychological safety one feels as a foreigner compels us to find connection quickly. Remember, our brains are always wired for connection and associate safety in numbers. Just as I mentioned with Christina, the brain says 'you're alone and exposed, you're lacking bio-energetic resources, go out and meet people.' This compels us to find a group of friends to form a safe tribe quickly. This tribe essentially sits in for our friends and family back home. As a result of this, connection is fast and exponential in its nature. You disclose much more about yourself with new people because, frankly, you don't have 20 years to make friends slowly, since you're only planning to stay in the place for two.

In a world where social isolation is now headline news, I argue that we can learn a lot from how people connect when they live a serial expatriate lifestyle. We can harness a bit of this bravery born of urgency to go out and connect, regardless of where we live.

Use commonalities to connect

Look at how much the global trauma of the pandemic has connected us. This one commonality gave us empathy toward one another in our shared experience. One of Christina Sang's favorite techniques to connect with others when she lived in Portugal as a foreigner who couldn't speak any Portuguese is what I call 'commonalities that connect.' 'I just found a point of resonance or a point of relatability. I'd literally be like, *Oh, well, you and I like food; all right, let's start from there. Let's start the basis of friendship building from there.* I'd go out clubbing, I'd meet some girls I don't know in the bathroom and ask, "Let's catch up and exchange numbers,"' she said.

Christina's technique of finding commonalities that connect is also backed by science and something called 'similarity attraction theory.' This states we feel more comfortable around people who look like us, our brain makes the inference that because we look similar in perhaps age, ethnicity, or gender, that we may share the same values and therefore we may form a friendship. In a room of strangers we'll also often be drawn to those we perceive are like us because it gives us a sense of safety, our brain subconsciously thinks these people are from our 'tribe.'

But what happens if you're like Christina, living in a place where there seems to be a big phenotypic difference between you and those around you? This week, try to harness the power of scanning for commonalities to expedite connection. Look for people in your day-to-day routine, or when out and about. Scan them visually. What commonality may they have as a point to start a conversation? The same leather jacket you own at home? A sports tee from your favorite team? Condition yourself to see the similarities over differences in our polarized world and watch magic happen. Then harness that expat bravery and strike up a conversation.

Audit your existing connections

Using the connection types discussed in Chapter 2, look at your existing group of connections. Are there people in the group who make you feel less connected? What bonds you as a group? Ask yourself: are these people happy for me? It may be time to refine whom you surround yourself with, to make space for new people to come in.

Let in a new tribe member

Are there people in your workplace or city who may be new? One thing that I loved about my parents was that they would always invite foreign students from nearby Murdoch University to our table. They knew what it felt like to be alone in a new country as immigrants themselves. It was so enriching for us as young children to learn about places we'd never traveled to, through the stories these new friends shared. Who could you create space for at your table?

Chapter 11

SERVE

Being
Others-Driven
in a
Self-Driven
World

From birth until age 17, when I went to live in Switzerland, I attended Catholic church services every Sunday. It is during the Mass that I was told over and over again about the power of giving to others. It is one thing to be a sassy 14-year-old sitting in a pew listening to this. It is another thing entirely to feel the true, profound, connective power of serving others.

As I gazed out the window of the same church building I'd later eulogize my father in, I'd see older migrant ladies – many of them what we call Asian 'aunties' – preparing busily in the church cafeteria. Removing delicately placed cling film from the sides of Pyrex dishes, inside which were homemade curry puffs and tea cakes nestled in paper towels. I'd look longingly at this, willing the priest to close the Mass so we could run out and get some of those treats. Dad would give me his spare change to buy things, and with a sweaty palm heavy with huge Australian 50-cent coins, I'd skip over the grass courtyard to the canteen. People would stay behind after Mass to chat while nibbling on their purchases, golden light streaming in on their shoulders as they jostled for the priest to come over and speak to them.

What I remember most profoundly was the passion with which these older women, their children long grown up and living in other cities like Melbourne and Sydney, would serve us. The money from these bake sales they painstakingly prepared would go toward building something new in the church, or helping a charity beyond the community. They would take my change and nestle clean, white napkins in my hand before placing a bright-green, sweet popiah roll called a Kuih Dadar in one or a crisp curry puff in the other. In the background, I'd see that this small canteen was full of ladies of all ethnicities – Indian, White Australian, East Asian, and Italian – swinging tea towels around their shoulders as they wiped down borrowed trays and cutlery ready to return to their owners. This is when I truly saw how powerful connection born of service could be. The simple act of putting out some food unified the families who stayed behind at Mass to connect. It unified the women by creating friendships, and this made me see the power of service far more profoundly than any sermon could. It wasn't religion that was actually connecting people in this scenario; it was the power of serving. The women were serving a greater charitable cause by baking and being in that canteen on their otherwise leisurely Sunday. My father was serving me with change from his earnings, and I was serving my family the treats I purchased, so they could stand in that courtyard conversing with the priest uninterrupted. We were all putting our egos aside to be of service to others in some way. Being intertwined in service is one of the keys to feeling healthily socially connected.

Giving to others makes us feel more connected to the tribe. We know that when we were early man living in these tribes, our worst fear was to be cast out. What better way to solidify your place in the tribe than to be useful to it, to positively impact it to such a level that you become indispensable? When we contribute to something bigger than ourselves, we feel more secure and connected. Therefore, being of service also gives us a greater sense of psychological safety. When we can impact our community positively, it's a reminder that we matter. If you're experiencing collective loneliness – a feeling of disconnection from a group with a like-minded purpose – then being of service could also be a way to find people with similar values and mindsets. You can make friends while helping others. It's a wonderful ecosystem of connection.

When Serving Is Your Job

But what happens when service is your job and you need to maintain your energy to show up for others daily? Kanitha catches the MRT (our version of the Tube) all over Singapore every day to make home visits to people who are struggling. When she isn't traveling between locations, she sits at her desk anticipating walk-ins – overwhelmed people who can no longer cope. When they finally decide to reach out for a helping hand, it's not at a time that can be pre-booked. They need to connect with someone urgently, and it's Kanitha they go to. She's often the final port of call for someone dangerously close to the edge.

She has been a social worker for six years and decided to become one after her own sister died at the age of seven. Kanitha yearned for a role model or a mentor as her family dealt with the trauma of the loss. She vowed when she grew up to ensure that others who felt forgotten, alone, or unsure of how to cope with their own trauma could get help through her. Kanitha describes her day-to-day life:

> *On a daily basis, most social workers have to deal with the most vulnerable and dark sides of human nature. One day a client came in expressing really openly that she wanted to kill herself. All I did was spend an hour with her – and I allowed her that space and time to share about the problems in her life, and she cried her heart out. At the end, she left feeling a lot lighter and even shared that just being able to have this conversation gave her faith that she could endure and continue the fight. I knew that that one conversation did impact her, and just knowing she had this lifeline that she could reach out to anytime, instead of feeling alone and cut off from the world, gave her the consolation and confidence to manage things on her own.*

Part of what makes Kanitha's work so powerful, and something that we can all harness in our own lives, is that kind of connection that makes people feel they truly belong.

It comprises communication where they feel seen, heard, and understood without judgment.

Connecting to the Tribe through Acts of Service

But being of service isn't, of course, just about making ourselves feel better; it's about actually helping other people. Shelly Tygielski is the founder of Pandemic of Love, a global, grassroots, volunteer-led, formalized mutual-aid community. 'Mutual aid' is a voluntary reciprocal exchange of resources and services, based on the principle that members of a community should feel responsible for caring for one another, and aspire to develop a community safety net where no individual goes hungry, without shelter, or feels alone. The organization started out during the pandemic as a Google sheet, matching needs with aid. Pandemic of Love volunteers were only mediators to match people. What makes the organization so special in human connection terms is that unlike a normal charity, people donating their time, services, goods, or money are in direct contact with the people they are helping, so they can see first-hand the positive impact they are making in the community. This makes both the giver and recipient of aid feel more connected. The giver gets a hit of dopamine and so does the recipient. One from impacting the tribe and the other from knowing they aren't forgotten. This was Shelly's response when I asked how she sees people change through being of service to others:

Connection is not a one-way street. In order for a connection to occur, two people need to lean in and make it happen. They have to be willing, vulnerable, and open to working through any obstacles or challenges that may arise, understanding that the outcome will ultimately be worth it. What I have witnessed through the connections made through Pandemic of Love is the fact that the emotional well-being of the individual being helped is affected just as much as the well-being of the donor assisting that person. Why? Because as much as it makes the recipient feel seen and heard, as well as obtain a measure of financial relief, it also makes the donor feel useful, capable of enacting change, and empowered to make a difference. I have witnessed how people who have signed up to be a donor and then truly committed to creating an authentic connection with the person/family they are matched with are forever changed.[57]

We instinctively know doing good deeds for others feels good, but it's also really useful in extracting us from our own sense of isolation. Service is an antidote for loneliness. It pulls the lonely brain out of self-preservation, offering perspective. In giving to others, we receive. It has been said a million times before, but may need reinforcing in the world in which we currently live, where being others-driven in a self-driven world is almost an act of rebellion. A life of success without service to something beyond ourselves eventually becomes hollow.

Serve People the Way *They* Want to Be Served

When we serve others, there's also an inconvenience to ourselves that allows others to be more comfortable. As I mentioned in Chapter 8, I saw this while watching my father communicate with his customers. He would connect with them in the ways they preferred. Kanitha sees this in her own work and shared with me her deep wisdom:

People always say treat others how you want to be treated, but I often wonder, why do we not treat people how they want to be treated? It's important to be mindful of what brings them comfort; because something entirely different could give you comfort... So pace with them. Journey with them. Don't try and fix someone on your own timeline. Allow them to go through their grief, allow them to go through their struggles, and then let them grow from it.

Vivian Pei is a food and beverage consultant, raised in the USA by Chinese parents. Viv is a service-industry veteran who started waiting tables in her father's restaurant at the age of 14. She bussed tables, hostessing and waitressing all the way through to working in restaurant kitchens in France. She experienced the thrill and joy of making others happy through service and serving them the way they love to be served on a daily basis:

I was working at CÉ LA VI as a guest chef and one of the waitstaff comes into the kitchen 15 minutes before last orders and says, 'Please tell me we have something vegan on the menu because we have these customers come in saying we have to feed them and all five of them are vegan.' As a cook, instead of just telling them to get lost, I just said let's look at what we can do for them. So, I looked at the menu that was there and the ingredients that we had, and we figured it out. We made them a very good meal... One of the biggest joys for me being front of house is to serve a guest in a way that makes them feel really happy. Sending someone off with a smile on their face. I mean, that makes me feel good.

There is so much we can learn from people who work serving others. Just look at our healthcare workers during the COVID-19 crisis! Yes, it's their paid job, but this joy from sacrificing for and helping other people lights them up in a special way that may not exist in those of us who don't work in service. I see this in the deep reservoirs of patience that my mother's caregivers in the nursing home have. How can we infuse the joy of an attitude of service into our lives, knowing that it helps fend off loneliness and isolation, adds to our sense of purpose, and makes us feel good in the process?

Service isn't just about the time we take to show up and do a charity project, and it isn't the sacrificing of money in a donation. It's challenging ourselves to be others-driven in a self-serving world and walking out the door every morning wearing that hat when communicating and connecting with others.

Volunteer, or do something good for others

As we now know, volunteering and doing good deeds are fantastic ways to make yourself feel less lonely, and they empower you. Have a look in your local community to see where you could volunteer your time. Choose something that appeals to your unique interests and talents, and you'll find greater opportunities to make new friends, too. Having a group of friends to volunteer with will make it more likely you'll contribute regularly as well.

Share your story and see it serve

I was part of school programs at homeless shelters and Indigenous women's homes as a young teen. The gap between the people I was serving and me was palpable. I felt awkward, steeped in my own privilege. How could I, in my middle-class, suburban home, relate to the trauma and abuse these women had felt?

However, as I grew into life, my father died, and Mom got ill. I now feel we'd have had much more to connect on. Certain things, like grief and loss, are universal human experiences, and in a bizarre way, these hardships, once processed, are gifts because they provide such fertile ground for connection. Kanitha sees this in her own work:

Sometimes it's difficult to convince people that there is a reason behind their suffering and pain. I do believe in vulnerability. I believe that clients will only trust us when they know we understand their pain. Where appropriate, I do share my own stories and experiences, just to show that I'm not on a pedestal. We all are humans here; we all have our own suffering.

Sit down and reflect. What stories do you have that can be used to connect with others? What were times in your life where you were hurting, and it took superhuman strength to get back up? Add these moments to your connection tool kit.

Chapter 12

PARADOX

Forging Authentic Connection in the Digital Age

You're going through a breakup. You've realized that, while you were in this relationship, you neglected your relationships with a lot of your friends. You sit there, scrolling on social media. You haven't posted in a long time. You post a quote about breakups. You get a like. You feel better. Your WhatsApp then pings with a message from a friend you haven't spoken to in eight months; they have seen your 'pain' posted online. Your brain fills with dopamine, the feel-good 'reward' hormone. This makes you feel better. Dopamine is addictive. It makes us feel great; it masks our pain. It numbs like a drug. You want more. You post again. The response feels good. You feel like you haven't been forgotten by the tribe.

More Disconnected Than Ever Before

We are using technology as a distraction from our loneliness. This behavior is particularly dangerous for teenagers. In an interview, author and speaker Simon Sinek describes how social media addiction can take us away from the real connection and sense of belonging we so desperately need:

We're allowing unfettered access to these dopamine-producing devices and media. Basically, it's becoming hardwired and what we're seeing as they're growing older, [is that] too many kids don't know how to form deep, meaningful relationships. Their words, not mine. They will admit that many of their friendships are superficial. They will admit that they don't rely or count on their friends. Deep, meaningful relationships are not there because they never practiced the skillset...[58]

Simon's words are backed by research. As mentioned earlier, the 2018 Cigna Loneliness Index, a study that spanned 20,000 Americans, showed that Gen Z (those aged 18 to 22 at the time) were the loneliest of all generations.[59] They registered 10 of the 11 feelings associated with loneliness, including feeling like people around them aren't really with them. It's a hard truth, but we're emotionally disconnected while having more access to each other than ever before in our history, and with the Metaverse being the next wave of where young people are connecting, we need to be cognizant of this. Susan Pinker, author of *The Village Effect: Why Face-to-Face Contact Matters*, writes: 'Digital devices are great for sharing information, but not great at deepening human connection and a sense of belonging.'[60] Technology alone doesn't quench our thirst for the connection we're wired to need. We have been using our technology in a way that makes us feel surrounded by surface-level connections, the virtual equivalent of standing at a party looking at all the guests and still feeling hauntingly alone. My greatest salve during the pandemic was seeing devices being used to engage with those we love in a more intentional way.

Using Technology to Emphasize Our Humanity

I'm a Xennial. This means I had an analog childhood and a digital adulthood. It means I still remember connecting with people without a phone. I remember when social media was MySpace – and I didn't even have an account there. I also remember the excitement when I got my first brick-like red Nokia in the early 2000s and saw text messages coming through. For someone who craved connection, my use of early social media, such as Facebook, was like a heroin addiction. Sending and receiving messages would send my heart racing, and not just when dating, but also when getting them from platonic friends. There were years of emptiness where my cell phone became a priority.

I still remember the first year I started thinking in Facebook statuses; it was 2010. I'd be in a situation, being with friends, and actively look for a quip, a quote, or a headline to post about. I stopped being present. At the time, I dismissed this as my 'creative radio brain' and that it was a blessing, that this was my job, and indeed it became my job. As a decade passed, the demands on radio presenters to 'up their socials' and post on the station Facebook became assurance to me that all this was a skill. Today, it's such a valuable skill that people pay to be coached on it. Most of my business still comes in through social media marketing. Maybe you found out about this book because of social media. So social media has its merits, but it's how we use it that matters most.

Being in the Moment

Almost a decade on, and I'm sitting across from one of my good friends. He's newly single. Another girlfriend and I have taken him out for his birthday dinner. At some point in the conversation, he picks up his phone and starts swiping dating apps. Right in front of us, while we're talking to him, averting our eye contact. He's in his late 30s. Just like me, he's a Xennial. I've known this person a long time and know he isn't inherently rude. We continue talking, and then again, any time he seems to glaze over, up comes the phone as if we, the in-person connections in front of him, celebrating him on his birthday, don't matter. I'm a little annoyed, I admit.

I think we get annoyed when we see behavior we don't like in ourselves mirrored in others. It reminded me of my time in Dubai when I was more interested in posting about what I was doing than enjoying the actual moment. When the engagement with my online following was more important to me than the people in front of me. Here, a decade on, this was karma. I was being what author James A. Roberts terms 'phubbed,' snubbed by someone else's phone.[61] Before speaking, I watch my friend and look at his body language from the view of a communications veteran. His head is down, his eye contact is non-existent, and his shoulders are turned inwards. Did the phone make him look like he had lost confidence, or was he actually not feeling good right now? When we're hunched over while using our phone, it gives off what author and communications expert Vanessa Van Edwards calls 'loser' body language. The inward-facing rolled shoulders and the aversion to eye contact are in themselves blocking any opportunity for in-person, serendipitous connection.[62] 'Loser' body language says, 'Don't connect with me; I'm busy,' to any passerby, the same way crossing your arms in front of you does.

'Are you OK?' my other friend and I both ask. He looks up and then spews a diatribe about how all the online dates were terrifying. I know the deep intimate loneliness that comes from seeing everyone else settling down. I was single for eight years before my last relationship. I know the deep pit-of-my-stomach, watering-of-the-eyes-inducing feeling of being hopeful about someone and then the rejection. For human beings, there are few things we fear more than the pain of social rejection. We equate that lack of belonging as meaning we're cast out of the tribe. What's scary, though, is where we once sat with this pain and mourned it, we now turn to our phones to numb. Like my friend, I wanted to keep swiping until the pain of rejection could be replaced by the excitement of opportunity. A possible new person who may fill the void of my not belonging and make me feel safe. I'd argue that we live in a world where there's so much ease of access to connections that three dates of something possibly authentic not working out can leave us feeling much more wounded than in that analog childhood of mine. This is for two paradoxical reasons.

Optionitis

The first reason we feel so wounded is that we perceive we've both seen a glimpse of 'everything that's out there,' but then at the same time, we have to keep moving and searching to find better options because the world has gotten more and more connected. For example, we can scan and swipe through a small city like Singapore's singles population within an hour at a dinner table, and when the right profile doesn't present itself, this gives us the perception that there's truly no one out there for us.

The other side of the paradox, which also makes us feel really alone, is our belief that there's always someone, or something, better out there. Without the internet giving us access to new connections anywhere in the world, our ancestors would date village to village, maybe village to city if they felt adventurous, but certainly, there was no clicking on Facebook to find the love of your life living thousands of kilometers away. We are now faced with 'optionitis,' the perception that our intended soul mate could be any one of 7 billion people on the planet. Now, because of the internet, many people feel a sense of obligation to find that person and not spend their lives with just someone they may have gone to high school with. I believe this overwhelming idea of options is yet another factor making us feel lonelier than ever. How can we possibly be mindful and present with what is in front of us when there's so much more on the menu to see?

This is because it means going wide instead of deep if you wanted to connect with as many people as possible. Our use of apps is advocating for shallower and faster romantic interactions in the hope of getting to meet someone better. This goes for dating, but also networking and communicating with our existing friendships. Chasing and searching for something better is leaving us breathless, and it's leaving us sitting at our birthday dinner, not making eye contact with the actual people who love us, who are in front of us, who want to connect with us. It has made us less present.

I lived this for years, so no judgment on anyone. I can speak life into it because for eight years of singledom, as dating apps had just emerged, I experienced the frenetic energy of it all. It wasn't until after therapy that I quickly learnt a lot of the time I could have spent healing was spent swiping.

Deeper Connections

Ten years ago, clicking into my Facebook was like looking at photographic proof of my 'cool Dubai life.' A world away from the messy, suburban house in Perth ringing with my mother's shouting. If my life looks like this now, I thought, if I've manifested THIS, then I'm safe from ever having to go back to being trapped in THAT life. Here, I'm loved. On this curated page of my own values circulating with the values and lifestyles of my friends who look just like me, I'm safe. This means I'm not crazy and unlovable, there are people just like me, and they are my tribe, even if we've never really spoken to each other in any depth.

This farce came crashing down when I went back to Perth when Mom had her stroke. Those wide, shallow connections will never hold you in grief. I needed to look up from my phone at the people who really cared about me. The ones who dropped flowers at my door on my birthday because I wasn't answering the doorbell and isolating in bed. The ones who brought me soup and food when I was single and ill and knew that I couldn't cook for myself. The ones who I could be vulnerable with. These are the markers of intimate connections. I'd argue we all need to look up from our phones more. Put the damn things away sometimes. I think we're on the edge of a mass awakening where people are craving time away from their devices. Maybe that's one of the gifts of the pandemic and its tech burnout. Many of us have just had enough of being held hostage by our phones.

Your device, however, isn't the villain. It doesn't have to be all or nothing with technology. Technology has an incredible propensity to connect us, as we've seen with the pandemic, but this is only if it's used correctly. I'm a huge proponent of using technology to spread not just the message of human connection but also doing the connecting itself. Here's what social media and smartphones can give us in the way of connection.

Use Technology to Enhance Your Life, Not Distract from It

Ray stands on the stage, it's the biggest presentation he's ever had to give in his entire career. He's been practicing for months and he's even had to memorize the presentation in English, his second language. The ballroom is lined with guests and bursting at the seams with some of the highest-profile businesspeople in Asia; the stakes for his new company ride on this speech. What no one knows in the background, however, is that Ray's father has been suffering from cancer. He's been told his father could pass away any moment now, and even making the decision to be in Singapore to give this speech with his father in Hong Kong is tearing him apart.

He gets on the stage and it's all going fine, but then there's a part of the speech which is about his grandmother, his family and legacy. He pauses, almost breaking down. It's a surreal moment to know what he knows and yet the audience is totally unaware. He keeps going and pushes through. When the speech ends he begins racing toward the airport but his phone rings. It's a video call, held up by his mother with trembling hands to his father in a hospital bed in Hong Kong. Through this video call, Ray is able to say goodbye to his father before getting on his flight. Without this technology, he would quite possibly have had to live in regret for his rest of his life. It's a cacophony of emotions I can well relate to.

When I was 19 and my father was dying of cancer, we didn't have smartphones. My mother's rare degenerative disease (which is literally eroding tissue in her brain as I write) means her short-term memory is fast disappearing. Five years ago, she forgot the days of the week and the times of day. Three years ago, she forgot my father died in 2004, and in 2018, the doctors said she would pass. She has not. Like all good, overbearing Asian mothers, maybe she's holding on to see me get married.

When I heard this news in 2018, my reaction was probably not what most people experience. I started filming my mother and documenting what I believed to be our last lucid moments together via my phone. This was all because I don't have video of my dad from 2004, as we didn't have smartphones then. Anyone who has experienced profound personal loss knows that photos only give us so much. Over time, I've forgotten his mannerisms, the timbre of his voice, and his smile. I wasn't about to let that happen to me for the second time, so I began recording my mother.

I began capturing so many moments with her in Perth on my visits and rewatching them when I returned to Singapore, reminding myself of our connection. Studies show that the simple act of watching a video of people we love can elicit oxytocin and make us feel better. Video has blessed us with far more emotional information to connect with than still images, voice notes, or text messages. However, there's no substantial scientific evidence to support that digital connection yields the same life-extending benefits of in-person connection.

After my mother had her stroke, she forgot her Facebook password. In 2020, on her birthday during the global lockdown, I was hit with a wave of sadness as her dormant Facebook account, still connected with mine, reminded me: 'Today is Sandra Heng's Birthday.' A small cake-with-candles animation blinked at me from the top right-hand corner of my Facebook profile. That Facebook account had reassured her that I was healthy and safe when I was in Dubai. She had made friends with my friends. She had gotten to see what my version of the Middle East looked like through my posts. Then the lights went out. We tried to get her password back, but the disease beat us during the process. Her condition deteriorated so quickly that she can now no longer even remember to charge her phone.

Despite this, social media is still being used in my mom's life. During the worst of Australia's COVID-19 shutdown, social media inadvertently became her lifeline to the outside world once more. If used with intention, technology can soothe those in the most isolated of situations.

Another Human Connection Superhero

My mother had been a teacher at Singapore's most elite girls school. She had regaled my sister and me with stories of her phenomenally high-achieving students. These women were Singapore's brightest and best, a nation whose education system is nothing to be laughed at. 'They wrote entire essays in poetry,' my mother would beam at us as kids, hoping the comparison would be made clear to us. Even though she taught there 50 years ago, it's still a huge part of her identity. She retains the memories of this time because they are long-term memories; in effect, this part of her identity is how she remembers herself.

After I posted a video of Mom for her birthday on my Instagram, the school reshared it on their alumni page. The next morning, the day after my mother's 72nd birthday, I woke up to these stories of connection. My mother at her best, like my father, an original human connection superhero. Here are just some of the comments:

- 'Mrs. Heng – Happy Birthday! You showed by example that we ladies can be anything we want to be. We borrowed your courage when we had little of it and grew into our own. I remember the time you confronted the flasher at the overhead bridge in Mrs. Sandra Heng-style. And not only did you remove our fear, but you empowered us to turn those situations around. After this COVID-19 situation, I will visit you in Perth. Stay beautiful and strong, always!'

- 'Happy Birthday, Mrs. Heng! I caught up with her about 12 years ago when I was in Perth.'

- 'Wow, she still speaks the same, her voice, diction, and mannerisms are the same since she was my Sec 2 Literature teacher in 1968. The last our cohort of 1970 caught up with her was during our 30-year anniversary in 2000. She was so sweet to fly down from Perth just for us.'

- 'Happy Birthday, Mrs. Heng. You taught us history in Sec 2/3 in 1970. A real inspiration to all of us. Great teacher and beautiful. May God bless you every moment.'

I called my mother immediately; I knew this would be the best gift for her self-described 'lonely heart.' As I read the messages to her, she sobbed. She felt remembered, acknowledged, and CONNECTED once again to the community beyond the walls of that nursing home, just as she had once empowered the voice of each of these young women and made *them* feel acknowledged.

There are a few things we can learn from this story about using technology to bolster our human connection. First, this incident had incredible connective and emotional impact on the women she taught. The connection spanned two continents: Asia and Australia, yet not one person met face-to-face during this story. It involved Instagram, Facebook, and a phone call. Devices used in the right way to give a healthy dose of oxytocin and dopamine to all involved. This is just one of many examples of how we can diminish loneliness for people we love using our devices.

Second, as a result of this interplay of technology, as you can see in the comments Mom received, some of the ladies will be flying to visit her. So using technology to create face-to-face human connection should be the aim. Last, like a happy marriage, technology and human connection should encourage and support each other. The digital should, however, always take a secondary role to face-to-face.

Dr. John Cacioppo from the University of Chicago clarifies it further by saying, 'If you use those [digital] connections as a way station... it's associated with lower levels of loneliness. If it's used as a *destination* – and ironically, lonely people tend to do this, they tend to withdraw socially because it's punishing, and interacting digitally, perhaps as a non-authentic self, makes them feel more like they're accepted. But it doesn't actually make them feel less lonely.'[63]

One of my final points on using technology to make us feel more connected is that, as Dr. Cacioppo mentions, we should be using it to show up as our authentic selves. Using it not as a highlight reel, as I did in my 20s, but as means of expressing our true values, beliefs, and vulnerabilities. Only then does it attract and connect us to others.

Use voice notes to augment your humanity

Almost all social media apps now have the ability to send voice notes as a direct message. Your voice has the power to change the life of someone on the edge. Communication isn't actually about you; it's about the person you're trying to connect with. Give them the gift of hearing your voice and hearing how much you care. How could you better use the voice note feature on your social media and messaging apps? Try sending voice notes more often.

Here's an example of how that occurred during the chaos of our March 2020 lockdown in Singapore. A local food delivery driver went viral when, amid the fear and grave uncertainty of the pandemic, he sent his waiting customer fully produced voice notes at 5:00 a.m. to update her on the status of her food delivery. He provided human connection when people were anxious and thirsty for it, and the story soothed us all. The voice notes were kind and warm, but they also had music performed by Yiruma behind them. Where drivers would normally allow automated text messages to update a client instead, Arif, the delivery driver, showed us a human was behind the service.

Be a present friend

In 2020, I started pre-shooting and batch-banking all my social media content so that when I was connecting with people in person, I'd be fully present. I decided to take images of my life only when it's a special occasion, not if I'm just doing a normal weekday catch-up with someone I love. I chose not to interrupt the flow of conversation to take pictures or videos of us together or our meals. Instead, I focus on being there and being fully engaged, leaning into those incredible, everyday moments of connection. It's the best way I've found to be present, while still meeting the social media marketing needs of my business. How could you create your own boundaries with your social media use that work for you?

Set limits on scrolling

In an August 2022 episode of *The Joe Rogan Experience*, Mark Zuckerberg (Founder of Meta) said: 'If you're just sitting there consuming stuff it isn't necessarily bad, but it isn't generally associated with all the positive benefits you get from being actively engaged, or building relationships.'[64] When I heard this, I almost fell off my chair, because it's a hack for my own time management and mental health habits I began implementing in 2019. We all know by now the mental health implications of scrolling too much and how the comparison trap can rob us of our gratitude. I love the creativity of making content. It's what I know how to do, but I don't scroll very often. I reply to comments underneath my posts, but don't go down the rabbit hole of scrolling my day away. Are you scrolling too much? How could you create a boundary for scrolling that works uniquely for you? Remember, most of us compare the messy back end of our lives to the highlight reel someone else posts of theirs. It's not real, and it's not worth your mental health. However, remember that for every hour you scroll, it's an hour away from forging real, health-boosting face-to-face connection.

Make eye contact whenever possible

Eye contact has got to be one of the most important things in using technology. It's important to remember that direct eye contact allows people to trust us more, and without trust, there's no connection. Human beings are skeptical of people who don't look us in the eye. When using virtual conferencing for work, put your camera on, direct your gaze to the small camera on the top of your laptop, and engage with the audience viewing you on the other side. An added tip, should this feel weird or uncomfortable for you, is to imagine the person you love the most in the entire world is behind the camera. This will engage a warmth in your eyes that primes you for connection and dispels the 'deer-in-the-headlights' look we get when we do something uncomfortable. (For more eye contact hacks you can use when virtual conferencing, see pages 207–209).

Chapter 13

REMOTE

Building
Connection
in the
Disconnected
Workplace

It's July 21, 1964 and Basri Sumanee, a young Singaporean Muslim man, walks to join 20,000 other Muslim Singaporeans for a procession to celebrate the Prophet Muhammad's birthday. As it always is in Singapore, it's a sticky and warm perpetual 35-degree Celsius day, a heat cloak of humidity surrounding him and his friends as they walk. At 4 p.m. the procession moves further into the city and Basree walks with his school friends. They stop at a street and see angry exchanges between Muslim Singaporean and Chinese bystanders. It isn't clear who begins the fighting. These fights escalate to violent riots, with bicycle chains, acid baths, and iron rods wielded as weapons of the everyday. The race riots spread throughout the tiny island's streets and they go on for months and deploy the entire police force. At the end of the first set of riots, 23 people have been killed. The fighting continues as the relationship between the two ethnic groups deteriorates, fueled by misinformation. The country is polarized between the 75 percent Chinese majority and 15 percent Malay minority. The riots were the worst violence this tiny island nation I was born in and now live in, ever experienced.

Singapore was a country and a culture disconnected. The four major races siloed into separate communities, speaking different languages: Malay, Chinese, Indian, and Eurasian. So how has Singapore now become one of the most profitable organizations, if we like, in the world? How, in essentially a few short decades, was a country fighting among itself able to turn the ship around?

First, the Singaporean government created unity through the commonality of language. By giving Singaporeans the communal language of English, the country was transformed because people could simply understand each other better. And the government made it mandatory, which meant students poured out of Chinese-speaking schools and went into English-speaking schools side by side with peers of every color. The government still allowed its people to retain their individual mother tongues of their respective ethnic groups and by retaining part of their own identity, they were also able to be proud of and acknowledge their uniqueness. We can see this now in how employees of organizations the world over are asking to bring their uniqueness and their own cultural, orientation, and other backgrounds to work while still being part of the organization's culture as a whole.

The second thing that the Singapore government did was it created a housing law that called for everyone to be given government housing, but then within this housing, the four races could not to be segregated. Through racial quotas, Chinese, Malay, Indian, and Eurasian would live side-by-side. We know through social penetration theory that over time, our need to be connected means we disclose more about ourselves with people.[65] This is much easier to do with people in daily proximity to us. Simply by being neighbors, over time, connection was created and the disconnection between the races began to close. Without this particular housing law, I wouldn't be here writing this book for you. This law literally created me. My father was a Chinese Singaporean from the majority race in the country, 75 percent. My mother is from the smallest minority, under 1 percent, a Eurasian woman. But the two of them were living in the same neighborhood because of these very laws created to build a culture of connection. They fell in love and got married, and they produced me. Without a culture of connection, I wouldn't exist.

Now, Singapore isn't perfect as a country. It still has issues with disconnection like any country in the world. But how far it's come in those short decades is an incredible model for how connection can be created. It's an analogy for how a disconnected organizational culture can be healed through the power of human connection, transforming the profitability and the well-being of people in their workplaces. We are facing a crisis in connectedness in workplace culture as a result of changes to how we work, be that fully remote, hybrid, or simply a lack of psychological safety.

I know what it feels like to work at both an organization with a culture of connection and one with a culture of disconnection. When I was 24 years old, I was lucky enough to be brought out to Dubai in the United Arab Emirates, to produce and present as a radio DJ for Virgin Radio in Dubai – it's this station that I mention in Chapter 9. You may have already heard about the Virgin group's incredible culture where fearlessness, innovation, and connection were part of the brand's values, both internal and external. As young 20-somethings, our team was encouraged and felt safe to try almost anything and if we failed, we'd learn something from it. Our number one responsibility was to be creative, and we knew we couldn't be creative without failing. We were hired for our diversity. Our team had every color to reflect the diverse audience we were broadcasting to. As a result of this, we were connected with the desires of our audience and could deliver a sound we knew they desired. This was back in 2009, and the organization's diversity was well ahead of its time. As a result of this culture of connection, we created some of the best content of my former broadcasting career.

So you can imagine my shock in 2015 when I moved to Singapore to work at another radio station, and here, in this organization, a deep culture of disconnection reigned. I had never felt so ostracized and lonely at work in my life. First, the organization had a very traditional top-down Asian work culture that was hierarchical. Hierarchy is embedded in our culture. A reverence for our elders, a respect for titles and rank, with business cards shared and received with bowed heads and both hands. Even in our language, when we refer in Mandarin to our aunties or our uncles, each of them has a rank. First auntie, second auntie, etc. Hierarchy is wired into us but at this organization, hierarchy took priority over creativity. People flagrantly spoke badly about each other, only to serve up cakes to the exact people they had been lashing to curry favor. It wasn't about how creative you were, but how you were seen to navigate the politics which saw you advance in the organization. In my team in particular, this came at the expense of the person who was bullied – a single team member who would be singled out and used as the communal point of disdain to bond other team members. During my time it was me, but I also saw the person who it was before me, and I knew when I resigned, explaining to HR that this was happening, that I hoped no one would be treated like that again. Those in leadership were feared and followed robotically, with no dissent to their faces but only behind their backs. Unsurprisingly, this disconnection affected our performance. Content was created that didn't talk to the heart of, but talked down to our listener.

I woke up one day bolt upright in bed, beads of sweat down my brow, and realized that employees who are disconnected from other people can't create content that connects because lonely people don't have a temperature gauge for their audience. They aren't even able to connect with themselves. This is what loneliness does to us. I was in such fight-or-flight from the toxicity of this environment that every ounce of creativity was a labor. Producing anything good on air five days a week seemed an almost preposterous request. I had insomnia, irritable bowels, and was totally disengaged with every promotion we ran. This seems so ludicrous to me now as a person who is hypercreative and writing a full-blown book for you. There is also good science behind why stress blocks our creativity and ability to solve problems and I'll share that later in this chapter. However, my strongest realization was, if this was happening in a small radio station on a tiny island, how were larger organizations who were trying to innovate products that could change our world being sabotaged by loneliness in their culture? And this is the same question, which needs to be answered in relation to the disconnection of remote and hybrid work.

A New State of Play

It's time for the whole world to accept that the way we were working pre-pandemic is never coming back. The hybrid tools that were birthed from necessity are so embedded, and so second nature to all of us after the trauma of COVID-19, that reverting to a fully face-to-face work culture is just not going to happen. This has been supported by the first large-scale study of a four-day work week sampling 33 organizations.[66] The results? None of the surveyed workplaces will return to the traditional five-day work week. Now there are many workplaces that have decided to go fully remote, and this has created its own sets of challenges, with employees uninvested in their organizations, just the way I felt in my last job. This also makes teams less resilient, feeling no emotional pull to persevere when roles become challenging.

Remote resignation is also so much easier to do because human connection isn't involved. In general, workplaces are being forced to assess their flexibility, workload expectations, and culture, in an economy in which Gen Z recruits are asking: 'What can this workplace offer me?' Just google 'quitting job on TikTok' – or, as it's known, 'QuitTok' – and it will yield countless videos of Gen Z employees quitting their jobs publicly as part of 'The Great Resignation'. Research shows that this wave of resignations has been caused by an aversion to burnout and a generational awareness that labor isn't what defines a person's value.

Human Connection is the Solution

So why do we need human connection at work? Employee loneliness is at an all-time high, meaning people don't feel connected to their workplace. Because employees don't have emotional buy-in with their colleagues, they therefore have no emotional investment in collaborative projects, which means they're not invested in the success of the organization at large. There is no feeling of working together in collective connection on a goal and these feelings, of course, are exacerbated by not having face-to-face connection with their teammates. The loneliness spiral perpetuates.

According to Fortune.com over 30 percent of remote and hybrid workers reported feeling lonely.[67] Similarly, a 2018 Gallup study saw that people who have a workplace 'best buddy' are twice as engaged as people who don't.[68] So, for organizations, employee loneliness equals disengagement. There's strong evidence to suggest that a connected culture is also fantastic for employee well-being. It reduces attrition rates, sick leave, and, of course, it increases productivity and gives people a sense of purpose. Connected teams are also smarter, more agile, and more creative. This is because human connection unlocks brainstorming power, which leads to more mental agility to solve problems and heightened resilience when stumbling blocks arise with a project. We literally feel like we have more support when we encounter challenges in a connected team, because our brain counts the people around us as providers of more bioenergetic resources.

For new employees onboarding remotely, there's also a void in the adoption of the workplace culture. Very quickly, loneliness can seep in and lead to quiet quitting. Workplaces need to adopt better hybrid practices if they want to attract the next generation of top-tier talent. Some of the problems cited by leaders I spoke to were managers feeling they had to check in all the time with employees to make sure they were getting the work done. This 'helicoptering' destroys trust, and we know we can't build connections without trust. It also created a productivity clog. Additionally, new hires felt they didn't know who to call on for the 'lay of the land' in their new workplace because, unlike the experience of in-person onboarding where it becomes very obvious through our innate human connection skills who may be an ally and who isn't, remote work makes this 'sizing up' process much harder to do. Again, for a new hire, this means a lack of trust, connection, and feelings of psychological safety.

There are plenty of reasons why I believe hybrid work can help connection versus remote or fully in-person options. We know from Chapter 2 we have many types of connections. With a reduced commute, parents can spend more time with their intimate connections and be less fatigued for their children and partner, for example. But remember, we also need collective and relational connections, and hybrid work allows access to those additional types of connection.

The problem many workplaces faced until recently was that no one had worked out how to do hybrid right yet. How many days should people be physically at work? I'd argue that the recent four-day work week study conducted by New Zealand-based non-profit advocacy group 4 Day Week Global gives us some good evidence to work toward.[69] The four-day work week may just be the sweet spot, with results suggesting that the four-day work week entices employees to stay in their roles by offering flexibility while also maintaining enough of that all-important human connection at work that's needed for great results. Corporations in the study were shown to be thriving as a result of the four-day work-week pilot, with participating organizations enjoying a whopping 38 percent increase in revenue.

So, if four days work well based on this new information, how should these four days at work be used and how can we create a sense of connection in this environment? Answers to this question may depend on your industry, and the nature of your work. Only time and more research will unveil the full picture, but here are some connection action points, garnered from business leaders I've talked to, that could improve the social cohesion of your workplace as we adapt to a changing work landscape:

Ask your people what they want

If you're a leader reading this, then put yourself in your employees' shoes. They probably won't tell you to your face that they disagree with how many days you want them back in the office. As we know, connection works best when we meet people where they're at. Use survey software to email your team and ask them to advise anonymously how many days and hours they'd like to return fully to the office and what they'd like to do while there. Aggregate this information to get a temperature gauge of your team and build your hybrid policy around this. You can also use this same tool to survey the office for common interests, be they foodies, sportspeople, or karaoke singers. Create smaller common-interest groups for socializing within the workplace and create monthly connection events around these.

Don't default to Zoom

People are also finding it hard to determine, in our adjustment to hybrid, whether a meeting in a calendar invite is for virtual or in-person. Label it in the invite and make it easy for people, but also don't make Zoom the default if your organization is struggling with building a connected culture.

Change how office days are used

Prior to the hybrid workplace transformation, time at work would be used for meetings and these were task-driven, not necessarily built around fostering human connection. It's time to re-think how in-office days are used. What meetings can be done online? Make the days where people return to the office worth their while. Make them productive not just for projects, but weave human connection activities into them. This can include team lunches, re-imagining the workspace by doing standing meetings, walk and talks in the green spaces of the office or its surroundings, or 'brown-bag' packed lunches where you have conversation prompts (there are many great connection card-decks for this available on the market – you can check out my YouTube for a review of them).[70]

Up your Zoom skills

We know eye contact helps build trust by eliciting oxytocin. If we want to present to and onboard new staff, we want them engaged and feeling welcomed. You can start by looking in the right place. Use the camera as the target for where to look when talking. I have many clients who read off a Word document on their desktop and as they do this, they are unaware that the tops of their eyelids – not their eyes – have center stage. This gives the person they're communicating with the impression they're averting eye contact and, as we saw in Chapter 12, human beings don't trust other human beings who avert their gaze. So, grab a Post-it note and cut a circle in its center; stick this at the top of your laptop screen so you can be reminded where to look. Make sure the hole goes over the camera so you can still be seen.

If all this still feels very weird and unnatural, remember my tip from page 193 and look down the barrel of the camera when delivering, as if it's the person who loves you the most in the entire world, to help elicit feelings of safety. If you're not just having a conversation or meeting and have to deliver a full presentation, take a look at the US-based start-up Vodium. us, which creates an in-built teleprompter in your device that aligns with the camera. This way you won't have that 'reading from my desktop' look when you deliver.

One of the other things I learnt very early on in my TV presenting career, some 20 years ago, was that the camera is simply not the naked eye. It dilutes 30 percent of all the things you love about yourself (your natural warmth and high energy) and seems to exaggerate all the things you don't like. This includes weight gain, sweat stains, and social awkwardness. This also means if you're naturally soft spoken, lower energy, and highly introverted, you may come across as almost disinterested on camera. So, here are a couple of ways to improve this:

Raise your energy by imagining you're about to do the thing you're most excited about in the whole world. We all have hobbies and pastimes we love. Channel that internal excitement prior to getting on camera to give you that 30 percent lift, versus just trying to talk abnormally fast or loud in an attempt to seem more high energy.

For added connection benefits, when others are speaking on Zoom, and you're in gallery view, it's OK to defer attention from yourself and look at the presenter's face so you can fully ingest what they're saying, then look back up to the camera when you want to speak. You can also give the same listening cues you would in real life, instead of just sitting there slumped at your desk, turning your camera off, or even worse, having the camera on but looking down at your phone or answering emails while they're speaking. Try to be an engaged listener. Nod to parts of what they are saying that you agree with, just as you would in person. Smile and react to what they are saying where it makes sense. This way, it gives the speaker social cues that their message is landing and also increases the chances your co-workers will be more engaged listeners for you at your next virtual meeting, simply through the rule of reciprocity.

The vulnerability huddle

A leader of a Fortune 500 told me about the 'vulnerability huddle' and I loved this idea. Let's stop calling the team meeting a 'meeting.' When someone says to you 'I popped a Zoom link in your calendar for a meeting,' it scares most of us into a state of boredom before we even go into the appointment. So, here's an idea, straight from the leader's mouth – change the verbiage around the meeting to 'huddle.' The word alone breeds images of connection and teamwork and during the weekly huddle direct the conversation to elicit vulnerability with these three questions:

- What went well last week?

- What do I need to do this week?

- What help do I need from my teammates to achieve this?

It's important that the team leader fully participates first, for subordinates to feel safe to share as well. Go around the team one by one, and make sure you're not excluding anyone in this exercise.

Phone-only Friday

As previously mentioned earlier in this book (see page 19), a study was published at the beginning of 2022 which stated that a sample of Americans associated video calls with higher levels of stress, and that audio calls created a greater sense of calm.[71]

When we're stressed, we can't connect well with others. So, try to implement a 'phone-only Friday' if your team decides to make Friday a remote workday. This allows them to do their household chores, walk in nature, or even multitask with their kids, untethered to a desk.

Remember as well that the smile is to the voice what eye contact is to the face. So, give that warm smile of enthusiasm when speaking on the phone – it goes a long way. In addition, move your head when speaking, as this helps to improve vocal dynamics. Sounding less monotone helps to communicate that you're engaged in what the other person is saying.

One-on-one walks in nature

If you're blessed to have a scenic workplace surrounded by green spaces, make those one-on-one intimate talks with co-workers less stressful using the magical grounding properties of nature. Remember, calling people into the office is now asking them to do the commute and can be seen as somewhat of an inconvenience. Soften the blow by taking them on a walk and talk if they've been brought into the office for the meeting. Of course, you can always use this tip for general catch-ups with team members too.

Chapter 14

TRANSFORM

The Future of How We Connect

Recently here in Singapore, I took my nieces, the daughters of my best friend, to my favorite casual Japanese restaurant. On Saturdays, this restaurant is bustling with people. There are small children screaming, running around while mothers rest infants on their chests. There are pushchairs and strollers jammed into corners. It's chaos, but the food is delicious. So, in Singapore, if the food is good, we'll brave any sort of discomfort to eat. You could be sitting outside in the rain eating a giant, smelly durian and if that fruit is good, you'll sit right there on a milk crate, plastic digging into your butt, monsoonal rain pelting down on a tent, and mosquitoes biting you, just to get that taste. What surprised me on this visit to this Japanese restaurant, amid all this drama, was that our food was delivered to our table by a robot.

The robot itself is simply an automated series of shelves on wheels, which runs up and down the central aisle of the restaurant and brings hot dishes steadily from the kitchen, allowing waitstaff to offload the dishes without running back and forth as much. They stuck adhesive eyes onto the front of it to make it seem more 'human,' but my two nieces found this absolutely terrifying. Immersed in this experience, my memory flashed back to my childhood in the nineties in Perth when Dad would make us line up in Northbridge on a Sunday for the best Hong Kong dim sum. I remember the line being so long that my stomach would be rumbling by the time we got to the front of it. And then when we'd finally get in, I'd almost be rolled over by aggressive Cantonese 'aunties' with carts. Everyone who has been to authentic dim sum knows what this is like: bamboo baskets humming with the smell of surprise treasures inside like hidden jewels waiting to be unveiled and lobbed in your mouth. And then my mother would yank me back to the table and say, 'Hey, hey, watch out, watch out.' Because the waitresses would carry in steaming-hot chrysanthemum tea in metal teapots while dodging food carts and toddlers at their feet, and all it would take is one child to trip up one of those women to get burns all over them.

Returning from this flashback, I begin to realize how fantastic the future is going to be if this is our present. Not only does the robot in the Japanese restaurant allow its staff to be less tired because they aren't doing the long trips back and forth from the kitchen – over a lifetime of service, that's saving someone knee cartilage. They can deliver more meals because there are more trays on the robot to house food than human hands can hold. They're going to increase revenue because they're going to decrease wastage from spillage and it's going to be much safer for everyone involved, with a lower probability of accidents. Now, I want you to imagine that our future is going to be absolutely full of things like this thanks to AI and automation. Already, on a recent trip to San Francisco, my tour guide pointed out driverless cars around the city center. You will no longer chat with people while filling gas; you'll no longer be talking to a taxi driver. It'll all be human connection-less.

This is already happening at another of my local restaurants (I adore Japanese food – let's get that settled first). I love the Japanese food court in a mall near my home, and especially my green chilli ramen. On a slow day, you get eye contact, and the staff see you. But this week, during busy lunch hour, no one looked up to greet me or anyone else for that matter. Imagine, before even entering, a server gives you a table number and a QR code. She taps into an iPad and makes the code match the table location. All this while never looking up from her device. She does this simultaneously for a family of four behind you and throws their code on another table. You order via another QR code and then wait for your food to come to you. There is no going up to the counter to order in person from one of the stands. You just sit, alone. Now this is just a taste of what is to come in reducing human interaction in our daily lives and we know from Chapter 2 that we need these micro-connections to keep us feeling part of a community.

Artificial Intelligence

Tony Tan, author of *The Future in the Present*, describes AI, essentially, as 'a computer program that learns to solve problems and reaches a pre-existing goal determined by its human programmers.'[72] And it's the backbone of these automated scenarios I've been painting for you. In the future, what may be perceived as 'low-value' tasks will be done by AI, which will then move any task done by a human higher up the value chain. We can see this happening already with the increased sophistication of new platforms like Chat GPT that can replicate human dialogue naturally. I believe this will increase our cravings for real, beautifully messy and deep conversation. In fact, studies already show that we perceive tasks done by a human being as more valuable. You can imagine that this means as our human interactions will be less frequent, our human connection skills will take center stage. So, if you have children right now, and you can make sure that they have profound social and human connection skills, they will never be out of a job. Don't just take it from me – Elon Musk was recently asked which jobs he thought will be safeguarded in the future and he said: 'If you're working on something that involves people or engineering, it's probably a good focus for your future.'[73]

The more tasks performed by AI and robotics, the greater the importance of in-person interaction. There are many pros and also many cons to this future. One of the cons that I want to share with you is that, for a lonely person, the interaction with a waiter or waitress asking them how they are, or giving them that oxytocin-inducing eye contact, that brush of the hand accidentally, could be all the human connection they are getting daily.

So, in this future, by you leaning into those human connection skills, you're also looking out for other people in your community who might need some basic interaction. You might be the saving grace for their mental health. We could see during the pandemic that, in stark contrast with social isolation, even a wave to your neighbor became loaded with meaning.

The Metaverse

It's amid this cultural context that we enter the Metaverse. The Metaverse as defined by experts Cathy Hackl et al: '...represents the top-level hierarchy of persistent virtual spaces that may also interpolate in real life so that social, commercial, and personal experiences emerge through Web 3.0 technologies.'[74]

If you have children who are gamers who use VR headsets, or you've seen them playing massively multiplayer online role-playing games (MMORPGs) like *World of Warcraft*, you'll have seen these metaverses with a little 'm.' Inherently, they are smaller virtual worlds. The Metaverse I speak about, with a capital 'M,' is already at our heels. In the Metaverse, these smaller worlds will integrate; there will be unique currency, economies, and an interplay with the real world. So, you could be walking down the street and through augmented reality, targeted pop-ups could come up on your phone. It will all be linked in a much more immersive way than what we see with social media and Web 2.0. And in this environment, we'll use avatars to represent ourselves.

Now, avatars exist already in current social media and gaming, and as a human connection specialist, this is what worries me about avatars:

Avatars

As a result of my mother's degenerative disease, she aged exponentially during the pandemic. Over the last two-and-a-half years, she has lost a lot of facial expression due to multiple mini-strokes. There's a total lack of dignity involved, because of that facial paralysis, a lot of saliva collects in her mouth. So, she's afraid to smile because she doesn't want the saliva to dribble out. What I've also seen is the decrease in the number of visitors she gets because they don't get the feedback that she's enjoying their visit since she can't express anymore. Looking at Mom's face now, I feel like she's being forced to wear a permanent pandemic mask that she'll never be able to take off. I'd argue this is the same thing that worries me about connecting with avatars in the Metaverse – not being able to fully have your meaning land; not being able to be fully understood.

The second thing that worries me about our future use of avatars, is how it will affect the developing social skills of our young people. Meta have currently developed a couple of things: one set of avatars that look like a cartoon, but match our facial expressions. Even if the avatar doesn't physically look like you, you can still get your meaning across. We can see this already in 3D-animation films, where we relate to giant pandas and dragons who express themselves like their human actors. They have also been working on photo-realistic avatars since 2019. Using your mobile phone, you can scan your whole body and all your expressions. Here, the avatar won't just look like you, but it will also express like you; it will show up and stand in for you. Mark Zuckerberg says he expects people to use the photo-realistic avatar for work and the expressive cartoon-like avatars for social occasions, like Metaverse parties and concerts.[75] So, your avatar will be like your outfit: you'll be changing who you are within the space, the way you currently change your clothes.

What concerns me here is that when I went into my VR headset, it was so captivating, that I, someone who is pro-face-to-face human connection, ended up in the space for hours until the battery ran out. This technology to connect in the future is so immersive and creative that it will also be very addictive. For young people who might not yet have boundaries on usage, particularly those who are finding their identity through the juxtaposition with others, they'll be defining themselves through this technology. The same way teens do now, using TikTok. How will avatars affect the future of how we connect?

It's a huge question, but I'm going to try my best to hedge at an answer.

In 2019, a 17-year-old Louisiana teenager, Anthony Templet, rings 911. In a deadpan voice, he says to the emergency operator: 'I just killed my dad... I shot him three times. He's on the ground.' In the 2022 Netflix documentary *I Just Killed My Dad*, we get more than just the audio from that call. As I sit in bed, indulging in my weekly vice of true crime, I can't help but be intrigued by Anthony's complete coldness. He is described by his stepmother as having a complete 'flatline' in emotion. His flat effect is actually attributed at first to a lack of empathy, incriminating the young man further – until the story unwinds to reveal, in fact, the exact opposite. Anthony is the victim.

Anthony's father kidnapped him at the age of five and moved him to another city, told his young son that his mother was a junkie, and that he was unwanted. Because the child was kidnapped, Burt Templet doesn't send his son to school. He tells people that Anthony was home schooled by his grandmother, yet the boy can't even write his home address. He doesn't know his birthday, nor has he ever been to a doctor. The parental neglect is criminal, and leads to the eventual homicide the documentary centers on.

However, there's something much more relevant to loneliness in this documentary that piques my interest and it's what Anthony does while locked away in that house with his father, with no friends or social interaction. Anthony plays video games. He is reared on them and in part, those avatars are the only 'people' he's socializing with. He's described by family and friends as always on his laptop or on his computer and 'real quiet.' In this documentary, I saw the beginnings of a social experiment that no sane parent would let their child undertake. Let's look at the conditions for human connection in this boy's life: a neglectful, physically and psychologically abusive primary caregiver, a lack of socialization, a lack of education, and unfettered access to video games for hours at a time, in which avatars provide the emotional connection for a child to mirror facial expressions. Avatars at that time could only have a limited number of programmed expressions (though, at the time of writing this, emotionally responsive avatars are being developed). In Anthony's case, however, he was literally learning from a series of stock emotions how to emote. Could this also be why Anthony Templet seems so wooden in his ability to express?

Our faces have many, many micro-expressions, but there are seven expressions that are universal across cultures, and we've discussed these earlier in the book (see page 144). Whether you're in Timbuktu or Zurich, these are the expressions that we're taught by our primary caregiver. We learnt to emote and to read emotion by mirroring this primary caregiver. Imagine if my mother, with her paralysis now had been the mother who had parented me for my formative years. How would that have affected how I expressed? And so those are my real concerns about the Metaverse. If a child is learning to read and replicate emotions from avatars for the bulk of their social interactions, this poses huge threats to their human connection skills. Skills that we know are absolutely vital to thriving as a species.

It isn't all doom and gloom, however. The good news for anyone who has seen the *I Just Killed My Dad* documentary, is the readiness with which, after his exoneration, Anthony begins to socialize and in so doing, becomes more emotive. Such is the innate wiring for human beings to be social: the muscle bounces back.

I have balanced views on technology. I've enjoyed the connective power of social media and there are many positives about the future in the Metaverse, too. One of the huge benefits of how immersive travel experiences are created via virtual reality technologies is that they could be life-changing for people who are paralyzed, like my mom. In fact, VR technology has already been used for the rehabilitation of stroke victims. Even in wheelchairs, people like my mom could travel again. Furthermore, for all those of us who've lived in multiple countries, I've often thought the only time all my best friends from each of those countries would meet would be at my wedding, or my funeral. But with the Metaverse, we'd all be able to connect with each other again, meeting with our photo-realistic avatars without the cost of flying, and still have a fun, immersive experience.

I do want to reiterate, however, that these immersive experiences will never be the same as in-person connection. Finally, here's the stark truth: the more time we spend using our devices, even now, the less time we'll be connecting in person, and that's the risk. So, how do we prepare ourselves for that future?

Here are a couple of ways to help:

Tech boundaries

Start using boundaries right now with the young people in your life, or with yourselves in terms of Web 2.0 technology. I have some really specific social media boundaries. I'm really active in the marketing of my business, however, I don't scroll because scrolling can be an addictive behavior. So, I post and ghost. In terms of regulating a child's device use, their internal boundary for this is taught by their caregivers. So begin to establish those; we need to set boundaries because there's no assurance that those creating these technologies will. How many hours a day is OK for your child to be on devices?

Micro-connection magic

One way we can get good at helping those lonely in our community, is by leaning into micro-connections now. Looking up from our phones when we're having our nails done or with our drivers in taxis, leaning into those interactions with our waitresses and waiters – how can you make the most of these moments?

Lean into your humanity

You will have noticed that this book isn't written in just plain prose. I use a very specific and uniquely human voice, I share opinions and I tell stories. These are things that connect us that AI can't replicate... yet. So when you're communicating, be it in text or in conversation, share your opinions, emotions, and your stories to augment your human connection skills.

| Conclusion

At the time of writing this, my mother turned 74. The night before, I opened my email with glee as my G2G pass to enter Australia was approved. Since COVID-19, Perth had become a bastion of pandemic-freeness and normalcy. People were basking on beaches maskless, and the government wanted to keep it that way. So, I applied for the pass, putting 'sick relative' as my travel exemption reason. They asked me, 'What are your plans for your travel within Australia?' I typed nervously, having already been denied entry once:

I will fly and stay only in the metropolitan area. After arrival, I will quarantine for two weeks in a government-approved quarantine hotel. I will then go to my local doctor for an Australian 2020 flu vaccine so I can enter the nursing home. I will visit my mother for the one week I'm there. I will be staying with an aunt and will also visit my godchildren. Then I will return to Singapore.

With its crazy, overpriced ticket and its longer time spent in quarantine than on the ground, this trip is ridiculous, but it is, like most irrational things, based on love. Deep oceans of love that I have for my mother. There is no one else in the world I'd do this for.

When they ask me to explain my reason for visiting, I want to say, 'Filial piety.' Can I put 'love'? Instead, I write pleadingly to be allowed in:

> *My mother has a rare degenerative illness; I haven't seen her since December 2019. At any moment, she could have a life-ending stroke. I wouldn't forgive myself if this happened, and I haven't seen her for so long.*

It's stark to be forced to write your anxiety down in this desperate way. The melodrama of it. Maybe Mrs. M. was right all those years ago in English class because it's highly likely an automated system is scanning my form and it doesn't care about any of my emotional reasons. There is no human connection behind this robot. Yet, how can it be dramatic or exaggerated when it's the truth? Black-and-white print on a form with a flashing cursor brings the situation into stark relief. Since 2013, I've been on tenterhooks thinking about the sudden stroke that could take her from us forever.

Connection is Love

The largest part of my healing wasn't just forgiving my mother, but learning who she was in her entirety. Researching who she was before I was born for this book and seeing everything she went through justified so many of her actions. She was ill and didn't know it; she was new in a foreign country, had no internet, and had her own childhood wounds. We often resent our parents for the things they did that hurt us, but that resentment isn't something you want to have in your heart when they pass. I'm so much of her that to resent her would be to resent myself. That's how closely we are connected. It took years, and sometimes it's still very stressful being with her, but I've always known that I love her deeply despite it all, and because of it all.

I'm not the only one who loves my mother deeply, who was wrapped up in her fierce charisma. I know this because when I returned to live in Singapore in 2015, I was inundated by emails to my website and social media asking me if I was indeed Sandra Heng's daughter and then with questions from her former students on how they could get in touch with her. These girls have now grown into community leaders; they are busy women. They must have seen me on TV, I thought. For all my wanting to put oceans between my mother and me, I still wore her on my face. I look just like a darker version of my mom.

Upon replying to these direct messages, these women called my mother to speak to her. Those still profoundly touched by her mentoring flew 4,000 kilometers to her nursing home in Australia to sit by her side. They bought my mother designer watches and scarves as if they were her own daughters.

Stolen Memories

For my first paid speech on International Women's Day in 2018, I didn't know any prominent female businesswomen personally to profile, which is what the client wanted. So, I called up my mom in the nursing home, and I asked her for the names of some of her former students so I could research them for the piece. She sat there clutching the phone in her remaining good arm, hunched with her breasts grazing the waistband of her diaper.

'Mama, can you tell me the name of the student you had who was the engineer on the Singapore train system?'

My mom pauses. 'Simone, I'm just so proud of them.'

'I know you're proud, Mom, but I need some names. What about the woman who was the CFO of that bank?'

Mom pauses a little longer. 'Simone, I'm just so proud of them.'

'Right, Mom, I know you're proud, but I really, really need names for my speech. What about the surgeon, the one that was a member of MENSA?'

I'm getting impatient.

This time my mother pauses for an inordinate amount of time.

'Simone, I'm just so proud of them.' Her voice breaks. A pause. My eyes water because I realize she's ashamed because she can't remember their names.

This story yields our final four takeaways on genuine, lifelong human connection. The first is the details of your achievements, what job title you have, or how much money you earn – in the end, those material accoutrements are so unimportant. My mother couldn't remember anyone by their job title. What she remembers and what matters, as Maya Angelou said, was how those students 'made her feel.'

My mother remembers the pride she felt for these girls and the inspiration they gave her in teaching them. There is an equal energetic exchange that comes with true connection. And that brings me to the second takeaway from this story: reciprocity.

Connection, Reciprocity, and Consistency

How can we tell a connection is authentic? Authentic human connection, to me, is reciprocal. The same way my mother was lit up inside by the experience of teaching these young girls, they were forever changed by the experience of being taught by her. Just as she never stopped feeling proud of them, they never forgot how she inspired them. So much so that these busy women would fly 4,000 kilometers to sit with her in a nursing home on their annual leave 50 years later.

In 2019, I had tea with some of her former students in a huge house in Bukit Timah, and photo albums were piled high onto the table. I saw my mother, much prettier than me, green-eyed and skinny-legged like Twiggy. In shift dresses and large glasses with short, curly hair. I often wondered what my mother had done for these girls to make them feel so connected to her. The answer is that she mentored them the way she parented me. She went beyond the student–teacher relationship. Their words:

- 'She asked us our opinion on things she wanted to buy for her home.'

- 'She invited the whole class to her new flat she bought with your dad. There she taught us to bake a pineapple upside-down cake.'

- 'She was fierce, but we knew she cared. She'd sit on her desk holding a ball of string threatening to tie our legs together if we didn't cross them like ladies.'

'Sounds like my mom,' I said, concealing my pride. Concealing my wonder, actually, because I had always thought her to be nicer to them than us. She was the same feisty, charismatic, and fierce mentor. She was consistent. Consistency – the third takeaway – builds trust. So if we want to build powerful connection, we have to put in the energy to show up consistently for people we love over the long haul.

The fourth and final point is that human connection rests on our humanity. To approach people, not through the lens of their occupation or with an agenda, but simply as our fellow tribespeople. You are human before you're any of the labels the world puts on you, from your job title to your roles as mother or daughter, father or son. She went beyond the student–teacher relationship to care for and mentor these girls. You can do the same when meeting new people – look past their titles, gender, race, class and connect at the deeply human level. Those basic needs that unite us – food, shelter, and love – are all great common denominators to speak on.

Human Connections Are Our Legacy

When you're at the end of your life, your children grown up, how you'll be remembered will be dictated by the seeds of human connection you've sown in your life. Your human connections are your legacy.

Human connection is at the center of almost everything we do; it's how we're wired, and a lack of it is the foundation for mental health issues like addiction, depression, and hoarding that we're seeing soar today. In these post-pandemic years, we're seeing awareness about the mental health crisis increase, and a yearning for face-to-face connection, and a recalibration of our use of technology. But by drawing attention to our need for human connection, I hope that we'll become more resilient to loneliness as a global family. In very plain language, if you want to be happy and live at the highest expression of yourself, you need healthy human connection.

We need love and belonging to grow into the best versions of ourselves, and the wounds from our childhood affect how we love and build relationships with others as adults. It's up to us to be courageous and reconnect with ourselves. The opposite of courage in this context would be to numb our pain. We can develop addictions when we soothe the pain of disconnection with behaviors like sex, drugs, alcohol, social media use, work, and more.

Sometimes the only way to overcome this disconnection is to be humble and apologize. I've done it many times, and I've been happier as a result. It has allowed me to move on with my life and invest fully in relationships, both past and present.

In connections, service should be at the center of how we communicate and love. An others-driven approach builds trust, rapport, and authenticity. Part of that authenticity also comes from unplugging from how we've been taught to show emotion. By expressing our emotions more fully in our words, in our bodies, and on our faces. Remember, when we show transparency, this tells others we're safe to connect with.

Quality over quantity is still the best approach when looking at your human connections. Cultivate depth first, as opposed to just a large superficial network. Remember, we need self-connection, micro-connections, intimate, relational, and collective connection to thrive. We can also help by looking at the lives of expatriates, following their cues for bravely putting themselves out there to meet new people, and learning to scan for commonalities when connecting in our highly polarized world.

Technology isn't going away; it's going to be a huge part of our future and how we connect. We can use it as the next best thing to face-to-face connection, or we can abuse it. Face-to-face, in-person connection still trumps all other modalities. Connecting with people well is the most valuable skill you can have in an era when people are thirsty for connection.

If anything in this book resonated with you, please let me know. I collect stories of connection from around the world. You can email me through my website www.simoneheng.com with anything you want to share. If this book has brought you to the precipice of understanding more about yourself, and this self-connection has prompted you to want to speak to a professional, I encourage you to continue your healing journey with the help of a trained therapist or counselor who has expertise in connection and communication and/or childhood trauma.

Lastly, I'm on almost all different kinds of social media and use the DMs to engage in heartfelt voice note conversations on the topic of human connection with many. Please feel free to find me @simoneheng on Instagram and TikTok or SimoneHeng-Speaker on LinkedIn.

Let's connect!

| Acknowledgments

To the Hay House team for discovering what was a self-published book, handed to you by trembling, self-conscious hands at your Edinburgh event, just the same way I had once handed my mother that English paper. You undid three decades of trauma when you celebrated this work and gave it a chance to spread from my part of the world to yours. Thank you.

Thank you to the wonderful thought leaders and authors who gave their time to blurb this book. Shadé Zahrai, Sue Cheung, Mimi Kwa, Steve Sims, and Shelly Tygielski. You were so busy with your own projects, yet made time to help me. That is genuine human connection through service.

Thank you to the interviewees who gave their time and allowed their stories to be featured. I literally couldn't have done this without you. Dr. James Coan, Shelly Tygielski, Helen De Rozario, Heather Hansen, Vivian Pei, Kanitha Jagatheson, and Christina Sang – I'm so grateful to you.

Thank you to the staff of my mother's nursing home facility. I'm continuously in awe of your patience and your hearts. Each of you is a living saint who has inspired many of the themes of this book. Thanks for making the winter of Mom's life the best it can be. I wouldn't be able to tell these stories without knowing she's being cared for all those thousands of miles away.

To the late C.P. I miss you every day. Thank you for being an exceptional human connector. Your story, in part, inspired me to write this book.

To Aunty Vicky and Uncle Muralee. Thank you for being my surrogate parents and helping my shrinking family when you had so much to deal with on your own. Thank you for giving me the space to learn who my parents were before I knew them and giving me the grace to process it all through conversation and a cup of tea at your kitchen table.

To Irene, my second mother, and a place to lay my head when the world gets too much. You are one of the kindest, most generous souls on the planet. Over the last 20 years, knowing I have your home in Switzerland to visit has given me a feeling of safety amid all the grief and loss. Thank you for always having your door open to the loud Australian exchange student two decades later.

To Paula, my best friend. There are no words big enough to thank you for being with me on life's journey. There were years and years where I had no one except for you. Thank you for being the absolute ground zero of trust, where I can say anything. Thank you for telling me to seek professional help in the most loving way possible. There would be no thriving and certainly no book without your support.

To my sister, Tamara. Thank you for being such a responsible sibling, so I could pursue such projects as this.

To my late father, Robert Heng, whose humility, grace, and kindness I try to emulate every day. You always knew how to treat people fairly, and you always put us first. I hope this book helps people see that there's such brilliance and wisdom in their local shopkeeper, should they take a moment to truly connect. I couldn't have asked for a better father. Thank you.

To my beautiful Mom, Sandra Heng. A lump rises in my throat just thinking how inadequate the words 'thank you' are in acknowledging the contribution you've made to my life. What would I be without you; how much less would I have done in my life if not for your tough love? I know, without a doubt, that you did the best you could with what you had at the time. I hope this book helps to keep the vibrant version of you in the world.

| Endnotes

1. Brown, B. (2020), The Gifts of Imperfection. Center City: Hazelden Publishing.

2. Sitt, T. (2018), 'What is Self-Connection?': https://www. freedomtomovegroup.com/blog-1/what-is-self-connection [Accessed 01/02/23].

3. Cigna (2018), 'Cigna 2018 U.S. Loneliness Index': https://www.cigna. com/static/www-cigna-com/docs/about-us/newsroom/studies-and-reports/combatting-loneliness/loneliness-survey-2018-updated-fact-sheet.pdf [Accessed 01/02/23].

4. Asatryan, K. (2015), '4 Disorders That May Thrive on Loneliness', *Psychology Today*: https://www.psychologytoday.com/gb/blog/the-art-closeness/201507/4-disorders-may-thrive-loneliness [Accessed 01/02/23]; Diamond, J. (2020), 'Loneliness: The hidden problem at the root of male irritability, anger, and violence', *The Willits News*: https:// www.willitsnews.com/2020/12/14/loneliness-the-hidden-problem-at-the-root-of-male-irritability-anger-and-violence [Accessed 01/02/23].

5. Holt-Lunstad, J., et al. (2015), 'Loneliness and Social Isolation as Risk Factors for Mortality: A Meta-Analytic Review', *Perspectives on Psychological Science*, 10(2), 227–237: https://doi.org/10.1177/1745691614568352

6. Curry, A. (2020), 'Ancient Bones Offer Clues to How Long Ago Humans Cared For the Vulnerable': https://www.npr.org/sections/goatsandsoda/2020/06/17/878896381/ancient-bones-offer-clues-to-how-long-ago-humans-cared-for-the-vulnerable [Accessed 01/02/23].

7. Hari, J. (2018), Lost Connections: Uncovering the Real Causes of Depression – and the Unexpected Solutions. London: Bloomsbury Publishing, p.71.

8. Lieberman, M. (2013), Social: Why Our Brains are Wired to Connect. New York: Crown Publishers.

9. Association for Psychological Science (2007), 'Loneliness is Bad for Your Health': https://www.psychologicalscience.org/news/releases/loneliness-is-bad-for-your-health.html [Accessed 02/02/23].

10. Austin, B.A. (1983), 'Factorial Structure of the UCLA Loneliness Scale', *Psychological Reports*, 53(3): 883–889.

11. Shaw, W., et al. (2018), 'Stress Effects on the Body', American Psychological Association: https://www.apa.org/topics/stress/body [Accessed 02/02/23].

12. Klinenberg, E. (2018), 'Is Loneliness a Health Epidemic?', *The New York Times*: https://www.nytimes.com/2018/02/09/opinion/sunday/loneliness-health.html [Accessed 02/02/23].

13. McLeod, S. (2022), 'Maslow's Hierarchy of Needs': https://www.simplypsychology.org/maslow.html [Accessed 02/02/23].

14. Hall, J., et al. (2021), 'Connecting Through Technology During COVID-19', *Human Communication & Technology*, 2(1): https://doi.org/10.17161/hct.v3i1.15026 [Accessed 02/02/23].

15. Fredrickson, B.L. (2013), Love 2.0: Creating Happiness and Health in Moments of Connection. London: Penguin Publishing Group.

16. Holt-Lunstad, J., et al. (2010), 'Social Relationships and Mortality Risk: A Meta-analytic Review', *PLOS Medicine*, 7(7): https://doi.org/10.1371/journal.pmed.1000316 [Accessed 02/02/23].

17. ART International (2017), 'What is Authentic Relating?': https://authenticrelating.co/what-is-ar/ [Accessed 14/02/23].

18. Sitt, T. (2018), 'What is Self-Connection?': https://www.freedomtomovegroup.com/blog-1/what-is-self-connection [Accessed 01/02/23].

19. Austin, B.A. (1983), 'Factorial Structure of the UCLA Loneliness Scale', *Psychological Reports*, 53(3): 883–889.

20. ABC Content Sales (n.d.), 'The Science of Relationships: The Secret to a Longer And Happier Life': https://www.abc.net.au/contentsales/programsandgenres/science-relationships-webtile/14089630 [Accessed 02/02/23].

21. ABC Content Sales (n.d.), 'The Science of Relationships: The Secret to a Longer And Happier Life': https://www.abc.net.au/contentsales/programsandgenres/science-relationships-webtile/14089630 [Accessed 02/02/23].

22. CourageousSpeaking.com [Accessed 02/02/23].

23. Coan, J.A., et al. (2006), 'Lending a Hand: Social Regulation of the Neural Response to Threat', *Psychological Science*, 17(12): 1032–1039.

24. Perry, B.D. and Winfrey, O. (2021), What Happened to You?: Conversations on Trauma, Resilience, and Healing. New York: Flatiron Books.

25. Brown, B. (2020), The Gifts of Imperfection. Center City: Hazelden Publishing.

26. Rudolph, K.D., et al. (2005), 'Need for Approval and Children's Well-being', *Child Development*, 76(2): 309–23.

27. Lee, S. (2017), 'Beyond Drugs: The Universal Experience of Addiction', Dr. Gabor Maté: https://drgabormate.com/opioids-universal-experience-addiction [Accessed 02/02/23].

28. Perry, B.D. and Winfrey, O. (2021), What Happened to You?: Conversations on Trauma, Resilience, and Healing. New York: Flatiron Books.

29. Perry, B.D. and Winfrey, O. (2021), What Happened to You?: Conversations on Trauma, Resilience, and Healing. New York: Flatiron Books.

30. Sitt, T. (2018), 'What is Self-Connection?': https://www.freedomtomovegroup.com/blog-1/what-is-self-connection [Accessed 01/02/23].

31. Kalogeraki, L. and Michopoulos I. (2017), 'Hoarding Disorder in DSM-5: Clinical Description and Cognitive Approach', *Psychiatriki*, 28(2): 131–141.

32. Hudak, R. (2021), '02. Hoarding Disorder: DSM-5 Criteria, Clinical Features, Epidemiology, and Comorbidities': https://psychopharmacologyinstitute.com/section/hoarding-disorder-dsm-5-criteria-clinical-features-epidemiology-and-comorbidities-2576-4959 [Accessed 02/02/23].

33. Heng, S. (2021), NEUROLOGIST Reveals HOW To Reduce Stress During COVID-19 Pandemic. [Video]: https://www.youtube.com/watch?v=0qRHLMqRIqc&t=2s [Accessed 05/12/22].

34. Heng, S. (2021), NEUROLOGIST Reveals HOW To Reduce Stress During COVID-19 Pandemic. [Video]: https://www.youtube.com/watch?v=0qRHLMqRIqc&t=2s [Accessed 05/12/22].

35. Murphy, K. (2020), 'We're All Socially Awkward Now', *The New York Times*, https://www.nytimes.com/2020/09/01/sunday-review/coronavirus-socially-awkward.html [Accessed 05/12/22].

36. Brown, B. (2020), The Gifts of Imperfection. Center City: Hazelden Publishing.

37. Blevins, A. (2020), 'Currents 006: Jim Coan on Our Social Recession': https://www.jimruttshow.com/currents-jim-coan [Accessed 05/12/22].

38. Holt-Lunstad, J., et al. (2010), 'Social Relationships and Mortality Risk: A Meta-analytic Review', *PLOS Medicine*, 7(7): https://doi.org/10.1371/journal.pmed.1000316 [Accessed 02/02/23].

39. Harvard Medical School (2008), 'Learning How to Say "I'm Sorry"', *Harvard Mental Health Letter*, 4–5.

40. Lazare, A. (2004), 'Making Peace Through Apology': https://greatergood.berkeley.edu/article/item/making_peace_through_apology [Accessed 02/02/23].

41. Lazare, A. (2004), 'Making Peace Through Apology': https://greatergood.berkeley.edu/article/item/making_peace_through_apology [Accessed 02/02/23].

42. Fredrickson, B.L. (2013), Love 2.0: Creating Happiness and Health in Moments of Connection. London: Penguin Publishing Group.

43. Fexeus, H. (2019), The Art of Reading Minds: How to Understand and Influence Others Without Them Noticing. New York: St. Martin's Publishing Group.

44. Van Edwards, V. (2017), 'You Are Contagious', TEDx Talks. [Video]: https://www.youtube.com/watch?v=cef35Fk7YD8 [Accessed 02/02/23].

45. Cuddy, A. (2012), 'Your Body Language May Shape Who You Are', TED. [Video]: https://www.ted.com/talks/amy_cuddy_your_body_language_may_shape_who_you_are [Accessed 02/02/23].

46. Robbins, T. (n.d.), 'Change your words, Change your life: The simplest tool for immediately transforming the quality of your life': https://www.tonyrobbins.com/mind-meaning/change-your-words-change-your-life. [Accessed 10/06/21].

47. 'Universal Facial Expressions: Are Facial Expressions Universal?': https://www.paulekman.com/resources/universal-facial-expressions [Accessed 30/06/20].

48. Russell, J.A. (1994), 'Is there universal recognition of emotion from facial expression? A review of the cross-cultural studies', *Psychological Bulletin*, 115(1): 102–41. https://doi.org/10.1037/0033-2909.115.1.102.

49. Marini, M., et al. (2021), 'The impact of facemasks on emotion recognition, trust attribution and re-identification', *Scientific Reports*, 11(1): 5577. https://doi.org/10.1038/s41598-021-84806-5.

50. 'The Real Health Benefits of Smiling', SCL Health: https://www.sclhealth.org/blog/2019/06/the-real-health-benefits-of-smiling-and-laughing [Accessed 30/10/21].

51. Lavine, R.A. (2016), 'How Eye Contact Brings You Together (or Pulls You Apart)', Psychology Today, https://www.psychologytoday.com/us/blog/neuro-behavioral-betterment/201609/how-eye-contact-brings-you-together-or-pulls-you-apart [Accessed 02/02/23].

52. Huffington, A. (2021), 'Creating a Hybrid Future Outside of Work': https://community.thriveglobal.com/arianna-huffington-reassess-relationship-technology-new-normal/ [Accessed 14/02/23].

53. Pinker, S. (2017), 'The Secret To Living Longer May Be Your Social Life', TED: https://www.ted.com/talks/susan_pinker_the_secret_to_living_longer_may_be_your_social_life [Accessed 02/02/23].

54. Khazan, O. (2017), 'How Loneliness Begets Loneliness': https://www.theatlantic.com/health/archive/2017/04/how-loneliness-begets-loneliness/521841 [Accessed 05/12/22].

55. Cacioppo, S., et al. (2016), 'Loneliness and implicit attention to social threat: A high-performance electrical neuroimaging study', *Cognitive Neuroscience*, 7(1–4): 138–159.

56. 'Dunbar's number: Why we can only maintain 150 relationships', BBC: https://www.bbc.com/future/article/20191001-dunbars-number-why-we-can-only-maintain-150-relationships [Accessed 02/02/23]; and Krotoski, A. (2010), 'Robin Dunbar: we can only ever have 150 friends at most...', *The Guardian*: https://www.theguardian.com/technology/2010/mar/14/my-bright-idea-robin-dunbar [Accessed 02/02/23].

57. Tygielski, S. (n.d.), 'Pandemic of Love': https://www.shellytygielski.com/pandemic-of-love [Accessed 30/10/21].

58. Crossman, D. (2016), 'Simon Sinek on Millennials in the Workplace.' [Video]: https://www.youtube.com/watch?v=hER0Qp6QJNU [Accessed 03/02/23].

59. Cigna (2018), 'Cigna 2018 U.S. Loneliness Index': https://www.cigna.com/static/www-cigna-com/docs/about-us/newsroom/studies-and-reports/combatting-loneliness/loneliness-survey-2018-updated-fact-sheet.pdf [Accessed 01/02/23].

60. Pinker, S. (2015), The Village Effect: How Face-to-Face Contact Can Make Us Healthier and Happier. Toronto: Random House of Canada.

61. 'Phubbing: An invented word that might be too useful to ignore', Merriam-Webster: https://www.merriam-webster.com/words-at-play/phubbing-words-we%27re-watching [Accessed 30/10/21].

62. Van Edwards, V. 'The Power of Body Language': https://www.creativelive.com/class/power-body-language-vanessa-van-edwards [Accessed 30/10/21].

63. Khazan, O. (2017), 'How Loneliness Begets Loneliness': https://www.theatlantic.com/health/archive/2017/04/how-loneliness-begets-loneliness/521841 [Accessed 05/12/22].

64. Rogan, J. (2022), '#1863 - Mark Zuckerberg', *The Joe Rogan Experience* [Podcast], Spotify: https://open.spotify.com/episode/51gxrAActH18R GhKNza598?si=b9Pei6veQX2VBrcDlpVNSA [Accessed 05/12/22].

65. Carpenter, A. and Greene, K. (2016), 'Social Penetration Theory' in Berger, C. R. and Roloff, M. E. (eds), The International Encyclopedia of Interpersonal Communication. Hoboken: John Wiley & Sons, Inc.: pp. 1–5.

66. Murphy, B. Jr. (2022), 'Case Closed: A New Study Says This Is What Happens When You Switch to a 4-Day Workweek', Inc.: https://www.inc.com/bill-murphy-jr/case-closed-a-new-study-says-this-is-what-happens-when-you-switch-to-a-4-day-work-week.html [Accessed 05/12/22].

67. Williams, T. (2022), 'Bosses are worried disconnected workers will refuel the Great Resignation. They aren't wrong', Fortune: https://fortune.com/2022/09/20/executives-worry-lonely-employees-will-quit-great-resignation [Accessed 05/12/22].

68. Patel, A. and Plowman, S. (2022), 'The Increasing Importance of a Best Friend at Work', Gallup: https://www.gallup.com/workplace/397058/increasing-importance-best-friend-work.aspx [Accessed 05/12/22].

69. Murphy, B. Jr. (2022), 'Case Closed: A New Study Says This Is What Happens When You Switch to a 4-Day Workweek', Inc.: https://www.inc.com/bill-

murphy-jr/case-closed-a-new-study-says-this-is-what-happens-when-you-switch-to-a-4-day-work-week.html [Accessed 05/12/22].

70. Heng, S. (2021), Review: The Best Connection Card Decks. [Video]: https://www.youtube.com/watch?v=UsnZPfiqHW0 [Accessed 20/02/23].

71. Hall, J., et al. (2021), 'Connecting Through Technology During COVID-19', *Human Communication & Technology*, 2(1): https://doi.org/10.17161/hct.v3i1.15026 [Accessed 02/02/23].

72. Tan, T. (2022), The Future in the Present: How AI Will Impact Your Life. Singapore: Partridge Publishing Singapore.

73. Shandilya, A. (2021), 'Elon Musk Shares Careers That Would Have Most Secured Jobs In The Future; Here's The List': https://www.republicworld.com/world-news/rest-of-the-world-news/elon-musk-shares-careers-that-would-have-most-secured-jobs-in-the-future-heres-the-list.html [Accessed 05/12/22].

74. Hackl, C., et al. (2022), Navigating the Metaverse: A Guide to Limitless Possibilities in a Web 3.0 World. Hoboken: Wiley, p.9.

75. Confidencial Digital (2021), 'Facebook Connect 2021 – Mark Zuckerberg.' [Video]: https://www.youtube.com/watch?v=pPp7oSJpCew [Accessed 05/12/22].

About the Author

Simone Heng is a human connection specialist and former international broadcaster for, among others, Virgin Radio Dubai, HBO Asia, and CNBC. With over 15 years of experience as a communicator on air, on stage, and one on one in different countries, connection has always been her life's work.

As a speaker, Simone inspires people to connect in a world thirsty for connection. She has spoken to thousands, and often for Fortune 500 organizations. Her clients include Google, Spotify, ByteDance, Meta, the United Nations, and many more. Simone and her work have been featured on CNN and in *Forbes*, *SCMP*, TEDx, *Vogue*, *Elle*, and *Harper's Bazaar*, among others.

Now based in Singapore – her birthplace – Simone was raised in Australia, has studied in Switzerland, and worked in the United Arab Emirates. She has a communications and cultural studies degree from Curtin University of Technology, Perth. This is her first book.

 www.simoneheng.com

 @simoneheng

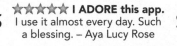

CONNECT WITH
HAY HOUSE
ONLINE

🌐 hayhouse.co.uk   **f** @hayhouse

📷 @hayhouseuk   🐦 @hayhouseuk

▶ @hayhouseuk   ♪ @hayhouseuk

Find out all about our latest books & card decks • Be the first
to know about exclusive discounts • Interact with our authors
in live broadcasts • Celebrate the cycle of the seasons with us
• Watch free videos from your favourite authors •
Connect with like-minded souls

'The gateways to wisdom and knowledge
are always open.'

Louise Hay